General Guide to

THE ISLE OF MAY

Fife's own Island of Mystery and History, Sea Cliffs, Sea Birds and Seals

James Allan

TERVOR Publishing
Scotland

First Published in the UK in May 2000
Second Edition, revised and enlarged, published July 2002
Third Edition, revised, published August 2007

ISBN 0-9538191-0-8

Printed in Scotland by
Barr Printers (Glenrothes) Limited, KY6 2RU

Tervor Publishing
11 George Street, Cellardyke, Anstruther, Fife, KY10 3AS

Introduction

Just where the Firth of Forth begins to turn into the North Sea, about eight kilometres (five miles) offshore from the nearest point on the mainland, lies the Isle of May. It is not a large island, as Britain's offshore islands go, but it is a fascinating one despite that. It is the largest of all the islands in the Firth of Forth, including Inchcolm, Inchmickery, Inchkeith, Fidra, the Lamb, Craigleith and the Bass Rock. With its dry land area of 45 hectares (111 acres), the Isle of May actually has a still greater claim to fame. It is the only real island with an area of more than 40 hectares that lies anywhere off the east coast of Great Britain.

Between the Orkney Islands to the north, and Scolt Head Island in Norfolk, to the south, there isn't a single true island as large as the Isle of May. Holy Isle (or Lindisfarne) is only a part-time island. It is cut off from the mainland by the sea only at each high tide. All the rest of the time it is connected to A1 arterial road by a causeway. Even Scolt Head Island is really only a shingle ridge on sand flats, a marginally detached part of Norfolk's marshes. All the other so-called "islands" in south-east England, such as Mersea, Foulness, and Canvey Islands, and the Isles of Sheppy and Grain, are linked by road to the mainland, so the first real island off the British coast that you come to, travelling south from the Isle of May is the Isle of Wight, on the south coast of England.

Vital Statistics

The geographical coordinates of the Isle of May are 56° 11.2′ North and 002° 33.3′ West. The island is 1,900 metres (2,080 yards) long, from its North Ness to South Ness, and about 450 metres (500 yards) wide at its widest point, from Green Face to Foreigner's Point. Except near the north of the Island, the shores are all steep and rocky, with impressive 46 metre (150 feet) cliffs along much of its south-west facing side. On the north-east side the shore consists of a long, low ridge of rocks and reefs, known in Fife as "skellies". Over the ages, geological upheavals have shattered the sill of teschenite rock which forms the Isle of May, and three distinct faults run roughly east-west across it. At high tide, the island is really divided into four parts. There is a small rocky islet at North Ness, then the island of Rona. This was linked by Nybo Bridge to the May proper. At the south end of the May, the area known as Maiden Rocks forms a fourth tidal island. Another prominent fault runs through the May proper, from Kirkhaven to Mill Door, but even at high tide, the sea does not actually divide this into two parts. Except close to high tide, however, you can walk dry-shod, from one end of the Isle of May to the other.

There is good fertile soil over much of the island. Some of this is sandy loam, some is rather crumbly peaty soil. Crops have, over the centuries, been grown here, and sheep from Fife were grazed on the May, at least during the summer months, in bygone days. There was, for a long time, a belief among Fife shepherds that the fleece of a sheep was greatly improved by a spell on the Isle of May. While the Benedictine Monastery was active (about 1150 until 1300), the monks kept rabbits as a source of food, and the descendants of these animals still infest the island, despite their population having been ravaged from time to time by myxomatosis.

In 1814, about ten acres of the May were being used to grow potatoes, barley, turnips, carrots and kale, and lighthouse keepers kept goats for milk, and cultivated a productive walled garden for many years. During the Second World War naval personnel stationed in the May augmented their rations from a substantial vegetable plot, and also reared a pig. (See also Chapter 6)

Changing Aspects

The appearance of the Isle of May, as seen from the Fife coast, varies constantly. Its colour changes, almost like a chameleon's, with changes in the light or weather. It can be just a black silhouette against a rising sun, and yet it can also gleam snowy-white in winter, almost like an ice-berg against dark storm clouds hanging over the North Sea. Some mornings, all there is to see of the May is a vague shadow, looming out of the sea mist, and other days the air is so clear it can seem to be almost within touching distance from the Fife shore. Its cliffs sometimes look dark olive, sometimes grey, sometimes white. Its vegetation changes colour with the seasons, from pale and dark greens to browns and yellows.

And its shape alters too, depending on whereabout you happen to be within the East Neuk of Fife, when you are looking across at it.

Seen from Elie Ness

Ask any natives of Elie, or visitors there, and they will describe the May as a long, low island on the far distant North Sea horizon. From Ruby Bay, or from near the neat little lighthouse on Elie Ness, the Isle of May is 15 kilometres away (8 nautical miles or 9 1/2 statute miles), due east. It looks, from Elie, almost like a small chain of islands, on one of which a stubby lighthouse stands. Especially in the light of the afternoon or evening sun, a white gleam from the shoreline sometimes makes it look like a little island of the West Indies or a coral atoll in the Pacific, with rollers breaking on its shining sands.

When viewed from rather closer, around St Monance, this almost ethereal vision has

Seen from near St Monance

firmed up into a more solid shape. The Isle of May still lies low in the water, silhouetted black against the morning light, or shining in the evening sunlight. Its most prominent features from here are again the lighthouse, clearly the highest point on the island, and a deep canyon that seems almost to split the island, just to the right of the lighthouse.

Come farther East, and between Pittenweem and Anstruther you are getting close enough to the May to be able to make out details, provided that the light is good and so long as the dreaded East Haar doesn't roll in. You can now identify the tall cliffs at the right hand, southern, end of the island, and from Anstruther

Seen from near Anstruther

you can often clearly make out the whiteness of the seabird droppings that have coated the black teschenite rock of these cliffs. The buildings of the lighthouse complex are clearer from this part of the coast, and you can see that these are on the crest of a rather steep-looking island hill.

Once you get as far as Cellardyke, the Isle of May can be seen to its best advantage. This is as close as you can get to it, on the mainland. It is just eight kilometres (4 1/2 nautical miles or 5 statute miles) from Cellardyke Harbour (or Skinfasthaven, as it is also known) to the North Ness of the Isle of May. The North Ness is exactly the same distance away from Crail harbour. Even without binoculars, many of the features of the May can be clearly seen from Cellardyke. The two prominent splashes of white, one at each end of the island, are the fog-horns. Another little white fleck, close to the main lighthouse, is the stump of the original beacon.

With the sun at certain angles, you can often distinguish the vertical lines of the volcanic columns of which most of the island's cliffs consist. (These are very similar to the "organ pipes" in Fingal's cave on the island of Staffa and the rock formations of the Giant's Causeway in Northern Ireland.) When the light is right, the way in which the birds' droppings have whitened these cliffs becomes very obvious. When a swell is running, spray from the breakers can be seen flying into the air along the shoreline of the May, adding yet more whiteness in striking contrast to the remainder of the generally dark-looking island.

As you travel the coast from Cellardyke towards Crail, the shape of the island gradually foreshortens. First, if you use a little imagination, it begins to resemble a WW2 "Flat-top" aircraft carrier, its sharp bow and flight deck to the west, and complete with a replica bridge structure and control room, formed by the main lighthouse buildings.

Seen from Fife Ness

Continue along the coast, towards Fife's

easternmost extremity at Fife Ness, and somewhere around Caiplie Coves you will see yet another Isle of May. The island has now become distinctly shorter and rather more rounded. At times it looks rather like a whale surfacing, as it swims towards the far coast. The tower of the lighthouse again adds to this illusion, seemingly masquerading as a tiny jet of water squirting from the whale's blow-hole. From viewpoints anywhere between Crail and Balcomie, the May begins to show observers its lower-lying, rocky, north-east coast. From these angles, the Isle of May no longer looks quite so remote and isolated, far out on the North Sea horizon. The coastline of East Lothian now lies directly behind it, showing you how much closer it is to you, than the town of Dunbar or the Torness nuclear power station that you can see beyond it.

From the East Lothian coast, between about North Berwick and St Abbs Head, the Isle of May can be seen as little more than a mysterious far-off island on the north-eastern horizon.

This more curvaceous and chubbier-looking Isle of May, as best known to Crail folk, is a very different shape from the one resembling a chain of tropical islands, that is seen from near Elie. The true shape of the island only becomes evident when you get out close to it in a boat, or walk around it, or even more clearly when you fly above it, looking down on all its cliffs and caves, grassy knolls and stony beaches, stacks and nesses, inlets and havens.

And well worth a visit it is too, either by sea or by air.

Seen from the air

Contents

Chapter 1
Getting To and Around The May

The Isle of May was made a National Nature Reserve in 1956, to protect its very special wildlife, especially the multitudes of sea birds that breed on the island, the many thousands of migrating birds that visit it, and its large population of grey seals. It is owned and managed by Scottish Natural Heritage. The island is also safeguarded by European legislation that is specifically aimed at the protection and conservation of birds.

The majority of summer visitors to the Isle of May (there are now over 6,000 coming to the island each year) sail across from Anstruther on one of the regular sailings from the harbour there. These trips generally last about five hours and allow up to a maximum of three hours ashore. This gives sufficient time to make at least a brief acquaintanceship with this fascinating island, although it is certainly not long enough to explore the Isle of May in all of its many aspects. That gives everyone a good excuse to come back to the May, again and again. There is always something more to be seen.

Sailings to and from the Isle of May

The sailing of the *May Princess* takes place at different times each day from Anstruther, depending on the state of tide. The landing facilities at Kirkhaven can be used by these cruise vessels, weather permitting, at most states of the tide. However, use of the harbour at Anstruther is governed by the state of the tide. It is only accessible for a few hours before and after each high tide. The trips to the May are also subject to cancellation occasionally, if the sea is too rough to allow a comfortable crossing and/or a safe approach to the anchorage on the May. Very occasionally a change in conditions means that, even after making the crossing from Anstruther, it may not be possible to land passengers on the island. Fog, however, is seldom a problem, as the vessels are equipped with satellite navigation and radar, and so can sail safely, even in very poor visibility. Quite often too, when the Fife coast is shrouded in the type of fog known locally as East Haar, the Isle of May can be basking in beautiful sunshine. For information about these sailings contact Anstruther Pleasure Trips, www.isleofmayferry.com (Telephone 01333 310103, Booking Line 01333 310054).

Members of Bird Watching organisations, yachtsmen, scuba-divers and other special-interest visitors will often make their own arrangements for travel to the May, and some information about this is contained in Chapter 9. The only accommodation available on the island is reserved for ornithologists (up to six in number) and bookings for this must be made in advance through the Bird Observatory bookings secretary (mwa.martin@btinternet.com). The Isle of May is normally closed to visitors in winter, and anyone wishing to land on the island between October and May should first contact the office of Scottish Natural Heritage in Cupar, Fife (Telephone 01334 654038). To make a trip to the Isle of May at times other than the summer months, special arrangements have to be made with local boatmen, usually either in Anstruther or Crail. The VisitScotland Tourist Information Centre (Telephone 01333 311073) in the Scottish Fisheries Museum, Anstruther, can generally give advice concerning the availability of such boats.

Facilities and Precautions

Even in the height of summer, it is always advisable to bring both warm and waterproof clothing. The wind off the sea can be chilly, and since much of the island is virtually devoid of shelter, a sudden downpour can quite spoil the day for anyone dressed only for dry weather. Most of the island is visible from well-marked paths, laid out for easy walking, so conventional sturdy shoes are usually just as suitable footwear for visitors as hiking boots would be. There are no refreshment or food facilities on the Isle of May itself (although soft drinks and snacks can be purchased on the *May Princess*). Near the path uphill from Kirkhaven towards the Tower there is an information building with toilet facilities, and a picnic area overlooking the landing place and old priory ruins.

Normally, a warden of Scottish Natural Heritage meets visitors arriving at Kirkhaven to explain the highlights of the island's bird life at the time, and to ask visitors not to wander off the network of paths around the island. One reason for this is to prevent you twisting ankles by stepping on fragile underground burrows made by puffins and another is of course to prevent you from crushing any poor puffins underfoot. During the breeding season, seabirds can easily be disturbed too, and visitors should then keep to a reasonable distance from the cliffs where they nest. Also in the interests of the bird life, no dogs are permitted to be landed on the island. For your own safety too, you should remember that cliff edges are not always as solid as they may look. A long fall from one of them to the rocky shoreline below could quite spoil your day out.

The marked paths allow visitors to walk the entire island, from Kirkhaven to the South Horn, with its puffin and grey seal viewing point near Lady's Bed, and back north again, by a variety of routes. Head along Fluke Street, perhaps, up Palpitation Brae, past the Tower, then Altarstanes landing place. The Nybo bridge has been removed by SNH to leave Rona as undisturbed as possible, so visitors should not attempt to cross West Tarbet to visit the North Horn. Or you can do the circuit in the opposite direction, with many optional little side trips, enabling you to see the Low Light and the North and South plateaus, or to return to Kirkhaven along Holyman's Road if you wish.

The *May Princess* normally approaches the landing stage via the north of the island, giving passengers views of the cliffs from around Bishop Cove and Altarstanes, then the low-lying areas of Rona. As you near the island, remember to watch the sea surface for rafts of puffins on the surface, fulmars in the sky above you, guillemots whirring along low over the water. You will often also see some of these birds plunge-diving for fish, and occasionally eider drakes and ducks, paddling along the surface with their ducklings. Often you will be able to identify grey seals swimming or basking on the rocks; occasionally some lucky visitors spot schools of dolphins or porpoises and a few fortunate people have passed close enough to photograph minke whales swimming near the Isle of May too. The return trip to Anstruther usually will, weather permitting, take you around the South Ness, past the grey seal colonies and giving superb views of the spectacular cliffs and sea stacks around Pilgrims Haven, the Angel, Green Face and the Mill Door arch. Even if heavy swell does happen to make a landing impossible, this sea trip round the Isle of May still is a worthwhile experience, and should whet your appetite to return in calmer conditions, when you can land to see the rest of the island's many attractions. And if you have spent time ashore, the return past the cliffs and stacks, the caves and seals, becomes an added bonus. Be sure you leave some film in your camera or some space on your digital memory card to record the magnificence of all this scenery.

The South Horn above the guano-whitened cliffs of Pilgrims haven

Chapter 2
What's In A Name

You may hear some local folk from the East Neuk saying that "Naebiddy wi' ony sense wid ca' it ither than the May Isle". To some people, "The Isle of May" is a name that was foisted on the May Isle by "foreigners" from the English Ordnance Survey, who didn't know any better, when they drew their maps of Fife. However, for better or for worse, the Isle of May it is, not only in this book, but in practically every other reference book, and on almost all contemporary maps and charts.

And who was this girl "May" after whom the island was named?

She didn't exist.

Nor has the island's name anything to do with the fifth month of the year.

There are several possible derivations for the name of this island. One of these claims that the May Isle name was originally recorded in the 13th Century as "Maeyar". This name bears a resemblance to the Gaelic *Machair*. *Machair* means a level or low meadow or piece of ground, and since much of the May is a sort of grassy plateau, some say that this could be the origin of the name. There certainly are many Gaelic-derived place names in the East Neuk of Fife, although these are outnumbered by names which have their roots in Pictish, Scandinavian or Germanic languages, occasionally combined with Gaelic. That is one reason I believe that another of the suggested origins of the May's name is rather more likely to be authentic.

The first of these alternative derivations is that "Maeyar" came, not from Gaelic at all, but from the Icelandic word for a seagull "Maer", coupled with the word "Eyar" which is said to mean "Island". Another theory is that the name was handed down to us from the Danish and Viking invaders, back in the 7th or 8th century. They called it the "Maa Øy" which is old Norse for "Gull Island", and sounds very much like the English (or Scottish) pronunciation of "May". So, it seems to me most probable that this book is really about the "Isle of Maa Øy". Either way, it is certainly about an island of seabirds.

Island Place-Names

Just a cursory glance at any detailed map of the island shows that there are many other local place names that have a history, either in fact or in fable.

Pilgrims Haven, Pilgrims Well, Monks Brae, Priors Walk and Holyman's Road are all connected with the presence on the island, according to tradition, of a Christian missionary, Saint Ethernan (or Adrian). You can find out more about him in Chapter 3 and Chapter 8. Other place names remind visitors of the fact that, for hundreds of years, the Isle of May was a centre of Christianity, in much the same way as Iona and Lindisfarne or Holy Island. These places include Altarstanes Landing, Kirkhaven, Chapel Field, Bishop Cove and the two impressive tall sea stacks, close to Pilgrims Haven, that are called the Angel and the Pilgrim.

Then we find Maiden Hair Rock, Lady's Bed, Lady's Well, and Maiden Rocks, all near the South Ness of the island. These names are all connected with the legend of King Loth, of the Lothians, who tried to kill his unmarried daughter, Thenaw, when he discovered she was pregnant. Want to know more? You can find out all about this story, and learn about its happy ending too, in Chapter 3.

Shipwrecks And Smugglers

At the other end of the island you find Mars Rocks, which got their name from a rather more recent incident, when the Latvian steamer *SS Mars* ran aground on the May. Some remnants of this wreck can still be seen around these rocks, though the main part of the hull lies offshore, about 13 metres under the water. That is only one of the many wrecks scattered around, not far off the Isle of May, some details of which are included in Chapter 8. These wrecks form just one of the attractions that bring many scuba divers here. (See also Chapter 9.) Foreigner's Point, at the south-east end of Island Rocks, got its name from when the Norwegian-skippered *Newcastle Packet* came to grief there in 1889. Island Rocks themselves are named after the *Island*, a Danish ship wrecked there in fog on 13 April 1937. Its skipper was on the last of his 260 trips between Iceland, Leith and Copenhagen before retirement, when disaster struck. Luckily, the Anstruther lifeboat rescued all 66 people on board. Some crockery salvaged from the wreck of the *Island*, and which bears the Danish Seaways markings, is still in use by bird watchers using the Low Light, and the remains of the *Island* can still be clearly seen from Holyman's Road.

There is a cave near the centre of the island's south-west flank, known as Press Cave. This name dates back to the 18th and 19th centuries. In these days, the skilled seamen from the East Neuk were regular targets of the Press Gangs, who skulked along the coast in Royal Navy vessels and seized local sailors, to impress them into His Majesty's service. They were hated and feared by all the local fisher folk, and on hearing rumours of their presence, seamen would take cover wherever possible, down secret passages, under trapdoors hidden by fishing nets, or in caves along the coast. The Press cave was one of these hiding places, used by men doing all they could to avoid being captured, probably never to see their families again.

Other caves along the south-west side of the May were almost certainly in regular use by smugglers around the 18th century. Merchant seamen would bring from France, Spain, the Low Countries and even America, cargos of wine, spirits, tobacco, silk, tea and even salt, all of which carried heavy duties. To evade the hated Customs

Duties, they would transfer these to local fishing boats, whose crews would then land them at isolated bays and coves along the coast. From there the contraband went to local merchants, who sold the goods, sometimes secretly, but often quite openly and with the collusion of corrupt Customs officials. The sheltered caves in the lee of the Isle of May were ideal places for the transfer from the larger to the smaller boat, and to hide the goods until the East Neuk coast was clear of Excisemen.

Several other island place names relate to the multitude of birds here. In season, Scots will find whaups (English visitors will call them curlews) around Whaup Rest. There are always plenty of shags, resplendent in their dark bronze-green plumage, at Shag Cave (as well as on many of the rest of the cliffs). But you would indeed be lucky to spot any peregrine falcons around Peregrine's Nest, though it still might be worth a try, given the enormous variety of bird life on this island. Over the past half century, well over 250 different species of bird have been recorded by observers on the Isle of May. It is this bird life that forms the main subject of Chapter 4.

Other Names

The following are brief explanations of some of the other place names not already mentioned or explained elsewhere, that visitors may come across on the island, or while looking at maps of the Isle of May.

Altarstanes	Named after the flat-topped rocks near this west landing place
Beacon	The original lighthouse, or beacon tower; now truncated
The Beacons	Two white-painted stone markers at the south of the Isle of May, used as guides by seamen entering Kirkhaven harbour
Black Heugh	The deep fault, the west end of which has been dammed to create the freshwater Loch
Burnett's Leap	The low wall on the north of the High Road at the steep turn on the descent to Altarstanes was built after assistant keeper Burnett fell onto the rocks below in 1889. He missed the turn in the darkness, trying to find where the *Newcastle Packet* had come to grief
Buss	The most southerly rock on the north side of the entrance to Kirkhaven. The sailing direction for Kirkhaven are "two Beacons in line, bear on the Buss"
Byres	Where Haven Road and Holyman's Road cross near Fluke Street, these buildings once were cowsheds or "byres"
Cable Cleft	Hollow leading from the High Road down to Horse Hole, near Altarstanes. This is where the WW2 loop cables entered the sea

Chatterstanes	In and south of Pilgrims Haven, rounded stones make a clinking sound when moved by waves, giving this area its name
Cleaver	A rock stack a few metres south-east of Lady's Cave, so named because it somewhat resembles the Cleaver rock at St Abbs Head
Coalshed	To the right of the path up from Kirkhaven towards the Tower, the building with vertical slots in its walls was the original store for coal landed at Kirkhaven
Craigdhu	Gaelic for "Black Rock". The rocky bluff on the north west side of the Loch
Engine House	Building adjoining the Loch
Fluke Street	Leads from the Loch to Byres, past former lighthouse men's houses (Allegedly after a similarly-named street of ill-repute in Dundee)
Haven Road	Leads from Kirkhaven to the Tower
High Road	Leads from Altarstanes to the Tower
Holyman's Road	Leads from the Chapel (or now at least from Byres) under a bridge near the Low Light and on towards Altarstanes
Horse Hole	The bay south of Altarstanes. So named after a horse fell into it and drowned
Iron Bridge	(or Nybo Bridge) The bridge built in 1938 to link Rona and the May proper was removed in 2006
Island Rocks	Rocks near Foreigner's Point, where the SS Island was wrecked
Loch	A small natural loch was enlarged by means of a dam here, to provide fresh water for the engine house and to cool the air compressors
Low Road	Leads from the Low Light to the High Road
Mars Rocks	North end of Rona, where the steamer Mars was wrecked
McLeod's Path	Connects the Low Light and the Tower (Named after a lighthouse keeper who was housed in the Low Light for many years. Some people use the nickname "Dunvegan" for the Low Light, from the ancestral home of the McLeods in Skye)
Palpitation Brae	See "Shag Brae"
Pilgrim's Well	Situated on the slope leading up from Pilgrim's Haven. The waters of this well were claimed to be able to cure infertility in women. (Suspicions remain that the resident monks may also have played their parts in these miracle cures)

Rona

Northernmost part of the Isle of May, where many grey seals breed. (Probably named after North Rona, the northernmost tip of the Outer Hebrides, which is a famous nursery of grey seals)

Shag Brae

The steep path from the engine house to the Tower. (The name has nothing to do with the birds of the island. It was coined by naval personnel who were "shagged out" after climbing it. Sometimes also called "Palpitation Brae")

Tarbet

The narrows between Rona and the May proper

Tower

The main lighthouse

The Loch and Dam at the west end of Black Heugh

Chapter 3
Myths, Legends and History

Geology of the Island

The Isle of May owes its existence to the volcanic nature of this part of Scotland in ancient times. Many of Fife's scenic hills are vestiges of old volcanos. Largo Law and the Lomond Hills are the most prominent, Kelly Law and the North Fife Hills are also remnants of volcanic eruptions. The coastline from St Andrews round to Leven and beyond, is full of volcanic ash and geological evidence of ancient volcanic vents. The East Neuk was a far from peaceful landscape around 280 to 350 million years ago!

Across the water, North Berwick Law and the Bass Rock are the most prominent evidence that volcanic eruptions occurred in the Lothians too, and it is not really surprising that the Isle of May turns out to be a massive chunk of rock known to geologists as teschenite. This material wasn't violently ejected from a volcano, in the way Vesuvius, Krakatoa, Etna and Mount St Helens have erupted. It seems more likely that, in its red-hot sticky liquid form, the molten rock from the bowels of the earth simply oozed into a giant fissure that had split the underlying bedrock of sandstone and limestone. This, of course, was long before Fife, or the Lothians, or the Firth of Forth, or even Scotland existed. Many thousands of millennia before, in fact. The molten rock then slowly cooled and solidified. During this cooling process the rock contracted and cracked into the spectacular columns of sharp-edged hexagonal pillars we can see today. These columns, with their prisms set roughly at right angles to the cooled surface of the original molten rock, are best seen in parts of the West Cliffs, around Pilgrims' Haven, and columns over 30 metres in height exist in several of the May's sea stacks.

Geologists describe the Isle of May as a teschenite sill, which is a technical term for a sheet of once-molten rock that originally erupted underground and then solidified there, deep below the surface of the earth. It may originally have been a reservoir of molten rock which supplied volcanoes that erupted at a higher level, such as the ones at Largo Law, Kincraig Point and Berwick Law. The sill that is now the Isle of May is now at the surface of the earth simply because the material that once covered it has been eroded away in the course of the hundreds of millions of years that have passed since the sill was formed.

The teschenite rock that forms most of the Isle of May is a harder material than the phonolite rock which forms the Bass Rock. The Bass is really just a plug of this phonolite rock that formed inside an old volcanic hill, the outside slopes and top of which have since been worn away by weather, glaciers and the sea. The softer material of the Bass Rock is riddled with sea caves along and below its waterline. There are some caves in the Isle of May too. Despite the fact that it is made of this tougher rock the sea has managed to hollow out several interesting caverns along the base of the cliffs of the May. Most of these started life millions of years ago as splits and cracks that formed when the hot teschenite cooled and shrank and have since been enlarged by the actions of the sea. Some of these caves are easy to spot while you sail round close to the island.

In the hundreds of millions of years since the rock of the Isle of May was formed, there have been many other upheavals of the earth's crust in these parts. Some of these have tilted the island, others have further cracked it. Comparatively recently (geologically speaking) it was, like all the rest of Scotland, covered several times by enormously thick layers of ice, grinding slowly across it in an easterly direction. Some scratches and grooves made by the moving glaciers can still be seen on rocks near Altarstanes, and on the cliff top just west of the lighthouse. These all indicate that the direction of movement of the ice was in an east-north-easterly direction. When the last of the Ice Ages ended, around 10,000 years ago, the ice melted away and it left the Isle of May in more or less the state we know it today. Many of its original rough edges had been smoothed off, and a useful amount of soil, carried across by the ice from other parts of Scotland, was left on top of the island rock when it melted. Evidence, in the form of "raised beaches," that Scotland raised itself up from sea level in stages as the weight of the overlying ice was removed can be seen in many places along the coast of Fife. On the Isle of May there is a distinct 50 foot raised beach parallel to the eastern shore of the southern half of the island. This feature provides the only decent piece of cultivable land on the May.

Before we leave the geology of the Isle of May it is worth mentioning that in several places along its coastline, you can come across quite large boulders of granite, gneiss, sandstone and other rocks that do not occur naturally anywhere on the island. Some are of material that is not found in nature anywhere in Scotland. Some such boulders have been incorporated into the Chapel and other buildings, others in the dry-stane dykes all over the island, but most were found in crevasses and chasms around the Isle of May. near the high water mark. Some of these may be what geologists term "erratic blocks" transported to the Isle by the ice and deposited there, but many are believed to have come as ballast on board fishing vessels, or from ships wrecked around the May.

First Inhabitants

From archeological evidence, it seems that the first human inhabitants of Fife arrived about 8,000 years ago. They certainly made some use of the island, probably fishing its waters and catching seals and birds for food. The earliest find made in archaeological digs on the Isle of May so far, has been a piece of pottery, probably around 2,000 years old, but ancient flint arrow heads and a bit of a polished stone axe have also been discovered. It seems possible too, that long before the dawn of Christianity the island may have had some religious significance, and been used as a burial place by our pagan ancient forebears. (See also Chapter 8)

Love Legend

The earliest story I have discovered that features the Isle of May concerns an illicit love affair that took place sometime around 515 to 518. The man involved was a certain Prince Ewan, the son of Eufurien, King of Cumbria. The girl he had seduced was Thenaw (or Thaney), the unmarried Christian daughter of the pagan King Loth, ruler of the Lothians. According to the legend, King Loth was furious when he discovered his daughter was pregnant, especially to the scion of another royal house. He ordered that she had to be punished for her fornication, by being hurtled headlong in a chariot from the summit of Traprian Law. But Thenaw, presumably landing on some soft ground, miraculously survived this punishment unscathed. Despite intercessions from the Christian element of Loth's subjects, following what they called a miracle, the King stuck to his pagan beliefs. His daughter's survival obviously proved she must be a witch. As such, she was now subject to death by drowning.

So poor pregnant Thenaw was rowed out from Aberlady Bay in a leather coracle, right across to a point not far from the Isle of May, and there left in the water to drown. Somehow, she managed to reach the Maidenhair Rock and to cling there to the seaweed growing on it. Eventually she became exhausted; her cold, tired fingers lost their grip, and she was swept away by the tide, continuously praying, and crying for God's help. Her prayers did not go unanswered, it seems, for she was finally swept ashore, far up the Firth of Forth, close to the Monastery of Culross. Here, as she lay alone on the foreshore, she gave birth to a son. Very soon after, mother and son were discovered by shepherds, who passed them into the care of St Serf, at that time Abbot of Culross. The son thrived, despite the inauspicious circumstances of his birth, and his name (or names, actually) are better known now than those of either of his parents. He grew up to become St Kentigern, later known as St Mungo, and was to become the Patron Saint of Glasgow.

But that isn't quite the end of the story of Thenaw, and her mystic escape from a watery grave. The anonymous chronicler of these events (in the Latin *Vita Kentigerni (The life of St Kentigern)* written around 1150) adds that, until Thenaw was rowed out of Aberlady Bay, it had always teemed with fish but that night, out of sympathy for her, the fish all followed the coracle across to the Isle of May, and when Thenaw drifted off to safety, the fish remained there. And that explains why, ever since 516, the waters around the Isle of May have been such a popular and lucrative fishing ground. By the time the 12th century *Vita Kentigerni* was being written, its author says, "there was such an abundance of fish that many fishermen from all the shores of England, Scotland, Belgium and France come because of the rich fishing, and are welcomed into the harbours of the Isle of May."

The Coming of Christianity

The first documentary evidence of people living on the May concerns the Christian missionary, St Ethernan. His name was later corrupted into St Adrian, and it is by that name that he is better known today. He is said to have come to Fife in around 840 as the head of a missionary band, to convert the Picts to Christianity. According to some, Adrian was born in Pannonia, which is in modern Hungary, and was possibly of royal blood. He resigned a local bishopric there, to undertake the missionary project that brought him to Scotland. After living and preaching in various places around Fife (including, it is said, the caves at Caiplie, between Cellardyke and Crail) he became the first Bishop of St Andrews. The name of Kilrenny, a village close to Anstruther, means "Church of Ethernan". Among Ethernan's company was another priest, Monanus, who is claimed to be the first person ever to have preached the Gospel on the Isle of May. Monanus did most of his work in an East Neuk village, then called Inverin, and which is the present day St Monance. Other authorities claim that Ethernan, Monanus and the other priests came from Ireland, and not from Hungary.

Around the time these first Christian missionaries arrived in Fife, in the middle of the 9th century, the local Pictish inhabitants were being invaded by the Scots from Ireland, under their King Kenneth II. The Picts were also suffering incursions from Vikings, sailing across the North Sea in their longships from Denmark, to raid and pillage. But the Picts hated the Scots invaders so deeply that they petitioned King Humber of Denmark to undertake an expedition against the Scots. The result was that a large Danish force landed near St Andrews in 870, ready to do battle with the Scots. By this time, King Kenneth had died and been succeeded by his son King Constantine II. As soon as Constantine heard about the threat to his Fife subjects, he set out from Perth to take on the invaders.

He met up with one Danish army, led by King Humber's brother Hubba, on the banks of the River Leven, and Constantine's men put the Danes to flight. The Scots then set off to track down King Humber, at the head of the other part of the Danish army. They soon found the Danes, who were occupying a strongly fortified position near Fife Ness. Constantine unwisely led his men in to an attack; the Scots were defeated, and Constantine taken prisoner. He was dragged into a small cave at Fife Ness by the Danes, and brutally murdered there.

King Humber then gave a general order to his Viking warriors to put to the sword all Christians in the East Neuk, men, women and children. It is said that about 6,000 people perished in this massacre, including St Monanus. St Ethernan fled, together with several of his followers, to seek safety across the water on the Isle of May, but the Danes followed him there. He and his fellow Christians were all murdered on the island, on 4 March, 875. His name was later enrolled in the Calendar of the Roman Church, in which Adrian's "day" is the 4th of March.

According to traditional tales, after St Ethernan (or Adrian) was buried in his stone coffin on the Isle of May, one half of his coffin miraculously floated across to the mainland, and this stone half-coffin remains to this day in Anstruther Wester churchyard. The other half, with the Saint's remains, is still, according to the folklore, somewhere on the Isle of May. You can find in Chapter 8, some information about recent archaeological digs, that have unearthed evidence of burials on the Isle of May, dating from around this time.

Pilgrims and Miracle Cures

The tradition of the martyrdom of St Adrian was so powerful that the Isle of May soon became a place of Christian pilgrimage for folk from all walks of Scottish society. A building was erected in Ethernan's memory, possibly on the site of earlier pagan burials, and for almost nine centuries, the Isle of May seems to have been used as a place of religious settlement. Excavations have revealed remains of an 11th century church which may well have been visited by the saintly Queen Margaret, wife of King Malcolm Canmore (1057-93).

King David I, in or around 1145, gifted the Isle of May to the Benedictine Monastery at Reading in England, and a priory was founded on the island. Over the next 120 years, the monks worked to complete their enlarged church, the Priory of the May, the Benedictine Monastery, and other buildings. A constant stream of pilgrims visited the May over these years, sometimes as an addition to their pilgrimages to St Andrews.

Other visitors to the Isle of May in this period were barren women from the villages of the East Neuk, and even farther afield, for tales of the miraculous powers of the

Reconstruction drawing of the Priory buildings as they would have looked around 1250. An interment is shown taking place in the burial cairn alongside the church.
(Illustration reproduced by permission of the Archaeological Unit of Fife Council Planning Service)

Pilgrim's Well had spread far and wide. Drinking of its water was believed to be a cure for infertility, and many a Fife child in these days owed his or her existence to a visit by the mother to the Isle of May. How much influence the drinking of Pilgrim's Well water had on these miraculous pregnancies, and how much the attention of the monks from the priory, is difficult now to prove. My own suspicions tend to support the theory that the latter was by far the more important ingredient of the cures.

Scotland's struggle for independence in the times of Edward I of England, John Baliol, William Wallace and Robert the Bruce, brought an end to the Isle of May's days of glory as a centre of religion. After considerable legal wrangling, the island was transferred from its English ownership to become the property of the Archbishop of St Andrews in 1275 or thereby. The Abbot of Reading tried to regain possession of the May, through appeals to Baliol, Edward and eventually the Pope, and it seems that the island did temporarily pass back to Reading after the defeat of the Scots in the Battle of Dunbar in 1296. It didn't remain under English control for very long, though, as it reverted back to the See of St Andrews after the Battle of Bannockburn on 24 June 1314, when Scotland regained her independence.

While all this was going on, the monks decided to transfer their Monastic home to Pittenweem, and the May became almost a deserted island. It was raided by forces from both the English and the Scottish warring sides, the church and monastery were demolished and much of the ornate masonry shipped across to Fife. Rabbits ravaged the landscape and the seabirds were left to breed in peace.

But, throughout the 14th century, Fife was quite a magnet for pilgrimages. The bones of Scotland's national saint, St Andrew, were kept to be venerated in the city of St Andrews, and there was also, in Dunfermline, the shrine of Margaret, the country's foremost female saint. Pilgrimages to places like these, and to such holy sites as Santiago de Compastella in Spain, formed a very important part of medieval faith. One of the popular pilgrim routes from the south crossed the Forth by ferry, from North Berwick to Crail, and these boats often passed close to the Isle of May. Consequently, many pilgrims coming to St Andrews and Dunfermline, also began landing on the May to visit the shrine of St Adrian.

Royal Visitors

Among the prominent pilgrims who visited the Isle of May were several members of the Royal family. Mary of Gueldres was one of the first, when her boat put in here while she was on her way from the Netherlands to Edinburgh, to marry King James II of Scotland. Later, King James IV became a regular visitor. His first recorded trip to the May took place in 1490, when he sailed down the Firth from Leith. He seems to have enjoyed shooting seabirds from a boat sailing off shore. There are records of him being back again in 1503, when he is said to have made an offering of nine shillings to the hermit, and to have paid his boatman, Robert Barton, five French crowns. Quite what an East Neuk boatman would be able to do with French Crowns, the records don't make clear.

The King was back again in 1505, visiting the May on 29 July and again early in August. An entry in the Accounts of the Lord High Treasurer of Scotland informs us that in June 1508, King James IV paid the May another visit, and that the sum of sixteen pence was paid to "...ane rowbote that hed the King about the Isle of Maii, to schut at fowlis..." James V is also said to have visited the May sometime around 1540, but there do not appear to be any records available to verify this.

During this period, the wily monks of Pittenweem stationed one of their number, more or less as a hermit, in the Priory on the Isle of May. Part of the old monastery was renovated around this period, and saw service as a hostel for pilgrims. The hermit monk's often lonely task there, was to say prayers over the relics of the saints buried on the island, to receive the pilgrims and, of course, to collect their offerings.

This went on, until pilgrimages to Fife began to go out of fashion during the 16th century, and in 1549, the Isle of May passed out of religious ownership. First it was feued to Patrick Learmonth, the Provost of St Andrews, and later became the property of many families in turn (including Balfour, Forret, Lamond and Cunnynghame) and of the Earl of Kellie. Early in the 18th century, the Isle of May came into the hands of the Scott family of Scotstarvit, near Cupar (and later of Balcomie, near Crail).

During this period a small village was built on the Isle of May. Anstruther church records indicate that the minister paid regular visits to the 12 or 14 families then living on the May. Some references state that traces of the walls of some buildings were still visible early in the 20th century although, strangely enough, recent archaeological digging has not managed to discover any trace of them. Some of the inhabitants of this village were undoubtedly fishermen, but others are said to have made their living from smuggling, and still others, prior to the building of the first lighthouse, from the deliberate wrecking of ships. The village cemetery seems to have been in a small hollow, near the cliff edge at the end of Priors Walk. Only one broken gravestone remains, and even it is not easy to see, being some way from the marked pathway. It bears the words "Here lyes John Wishart husband to Euphan Horsborough who lived on the island of May who died in March the 3 1730 aged 45". He was probably the final person in long line, stretching back possibly to the Bronze Age, over 3,000 years ago, to have been buried on the island.

There are some suggestions that yet another "King James" may have visited the Isle of May, early in 1716. How this came about is described later, in Chapter 7.

In 1815, the Commissioners of Northern Lights purchased the Isle of May from the Scott family, for the sum of £60,000 and it remained in the hands of this Northern Lighthouse Board until 1988. During this period, in 1956, the island was made a National Nature Reserve with the aim of protecting its very special wildlife. In 1988 it became the property of Scottish Natural Heritage, who now own and manage it. Scottish Natural Heritage is an independent government agency, responsible for safeguarding and enhancing Scotland's natural heritage, promoting the understanding and enjoyment thereof, and ensuring that it is used wisely.

Tragedy of the *Johns*

One sad episode in the history of the Isle of May is still etched in the memories of many people of the East Neuk villages. Each summer, an excursion was undertaken from the mainland to the May, an event looked forward to eagerly for months, and always accompanied by a great deal of merry-making and dancing. In 1837, the annual outing to the May took place on Saturday 1 July, and among the five vessels that set out from Anstruther was the *Johns*, with 65 people on board. The sea was calm, sparkling in the summer sunshine and all went well until the *Johns* was entering Kirkhaven harbour. Then, for some still unexplained reason, the boat struck a rock. The passengers panicked, rushed to one side of the boat, and the *Johns* capsized, throwing all the holiday makers into the water. Thirteen lives were lost. Her skipper was acquitted of a charge of culpable homicide (for "having landed at Kirkhaven instead of Altarstanes and for having used four oars instead of eight") but the annual outing to the May never again took place.

Between 1907 and 1933, two ladies, the Misses Baxter and Rintoul did a great deal of work on the Isle of May concerning the study of bird migration. Then in September 1934 a Bird Observatory was established on the Island, only the second such observatory in the United Kingdom, following that on Skokholm Island, off the Welsh coast that was set up in 1933.

I have also met a frequent visitor to the Isle of May who claims to have encountered the ghost of the Isle of May. On at least two occasions he, and others occupying the quarters at the Low Light, have been disturbed late at night by the sound of footsteps coming down McLeod's Path towards the building. They have then seen a shadowy figure pass the window, but just when they expect someone to come in the door, there is silence. They have gone outside and looked around, but found no one; nothing. Yet McLeod's Path ends at the Low Light, and anyone coming down it must either return past the window, or disappear into the sea at Tarbet Hole. The lighthouse men, the only other souls on the island, confirmed that they hadn't been outside their quarters on either occasion. So the men and women who were in the Low Light are quite convinced they have heard and seen a paranormal apparition. The ghost of some poor drowned soul from the *Johns*, perhaps; or a lost submariner; the restless spirit of an airman from one of the many aeroplane ditchings in the sea near the May; the phantom of the lonely villager buried under the May's solitary broken tombstone, or... who knows?

McLeod's Path leading to the Low Light, seen from the lantern of the main lighthouse.

Chapter 4
Feathered Friends

There are several excellent specialist books about the immense variety of bird life that exists on the Isle of May. It is not my intention here to duplicate what these publications cover, so ornithologists will find little that is new to them in this Chapter. My aim here is simply to give readers who are interested in birds but who are not specialists, a brief idea of what they are likely to see on, and flying over, the island.

Since observations of birds began on the Isle of May, well over 250 different species have been identified here. This extraordinary variety includes both the native birds which breed here, and the large numbers of migratory species which use the May as a staging post at differing times of the year.

Altogether the Isle of May has a population of somewhere around 100,000 birds during the period between March and July. The main species that breed on the May include the following, arranged more or less in decreasing sizes of their local populations:

puffins, guillemots, kittiwakes, herring gulls, lesser black-backed gulls, shags, razorbills, eider ducks, fulmars, common terns, and oystercatchers.

Other species that have been known to breed on the May in recent years (although in smaller numbers) include:

arctic terns, lapwings, wild pigeons, starlings, swallows, pied wagtails, rock pipits, meadow pipits, great black-backed gulls, blackbirds, song thrushes, linnets and crows.

Up to date information about bird life on the Island is available on: http://isleofmaybirdobs.mysite.wanadoo-members.co.uk

Fluctuating Numbers

The numbers of each species do tend to vary greatly from year to year, as changes in environment, food supply, weather, disease and natural enemies take place. Huge increases in the herring gull population of the May in the 1970s, for instance, caused the terns almost to die out, due to gulls attacking their nests and chicks. It became necessary to control the number of gulls breeding on the May, in order to protect the terns and also to stop the gulls causing erosion of the soil, by destroying much of the island's vegetation. This cull, and the destruction of herring gull nests, has reduced their numbers to more manageable proportions, and allowed the terns to return to breed on the May again. At the end of WW2, there were vast numbers of terns on the island. At that time over 10,000 common terns and 3,000 Sandwich terns, together with smaller numbers of Arctic terns and a few roseate terns, all bred on the Isle of May. During the gull domination, their numbers had dwindled to just a dozen or so common terns, but the tern population is now on the increase again.

Similarly, some years ago, the population of shags dropped to well under 1,000 as a result of many adult shags being poisoned by eating shellfish contaminated by algae. Natural changes since then have seen the number of shags on the May increase to around four times that number.

It is thus, obviously, impossible to say from one year to another, just how many of any particular bird are going to be on the Isle of May for visitors to see. What is certain, though, is that, barring some unforseen disaster like a major oil-spill, the May's reputation as a paradise for bird watching, is likely to endure for many years to come. Visitors can find out from the Warden of Scottish Natural Heritage, who meets each boat as it comes in, just which birds are most likely to be around at the time of their visit. Information is also usually available at the visitor centre, near the Kirkhaven landing.

Popular Puffins

The most popular bird with many visitors is the puffin. This is a comical little chap to watch, with a brightly-coloured orange-red beak and a smart plumage, reminiscent of a black dinner jacket and white shirt. On the ground,

Puffins

they waddle about in rather an awkward manner, but in the air they are magnificent flyers. They use their huge orange bill to gather and bring home food for their brood, sand-eels and other small fish. Sometimes you see a puffin, with its fishy food supply sticking out either side of its beak, being attacked in mid-air by gulls. They seem to find it easier to steal the puffin's food for its family, than to fish for themselves. The puffins breed in burrows and spend much of the breeding season between April and July, underground. However, at least a few can usually be seen at any time, somewhere on the island.

It is mainly because of this burrowing habit of the puffins, that visitors are urged to keep only to the defined paths on the Isle of May. Wander anywhere else, and you are liable not only to disturb wildlife, but to walk on parts where the soil is dangerously fragile, not to mention the very real risk of crushing poor innocent puffins underfoot.

In late March and early April, and after the breeding season ends, in about mid-July, puffins are to be found all over the island. At times the air can be thick with puffins in places, their wings positively whirring as they circle around their nesting areas, for all the world like a huge swarm of bees.

Shags and Cormorants

Among the most striking of the birds on the Isle of May are the shags. Many visitors, on seeing these handsome big creatures, immediately call them cormorants, but that, according to the bird experts, they are not. There is a well-known piece of doggerel that starts:

> The common cormorant or shag
> Lays eggs inside a paper bag.
> The reason, you will see, no doubt -
> It is to keep the lightning out....

and, perhaps because of hearing this nonsense poem when a child, the false idea took root in my mind (and probably in the minds of many other people too) that shags and cormorants are one and the same. There are, however, very few cormorants on the Isle of May. Almost all of these large, dark bronze-green plumaged birds with the long, snake-like necks, yellow tinged beaks and rubbery-looking webbed feet, are shags. They

Shag drying its wings

are slightly smaller than cormorants, lack the white patches on face and thighs, that are always to be seen on cormorants, and have more of a greenish tinge to their dark feathers than the blue hue of the cormorant's plumage.

If you manage to visit the May early enough in the year, you will be able to see how the shags wear tufts of feathers on their foreheads, which no self-respecting cormorant ever does. I feel these crests do tend to make shags look a trifle odd while wearing them, but they soon disappear, being shed generally about the time that the shags start sitting on their eggs. Shags nest all around the cliffs of the Isle of May, and their nests can be wonderfully untidy constructions of sticks and seaweed, plastic bottles and tin

Shags in flight

cans, bits of rope and any old flotsam that takes their fancy. If you fancy taking some photographs of these shags, you scarcely need a telephoto lens. Most of them are tame enough to let you come reasonably close. Male and female look much the same to human eyes, but females tend to give themselves away, when agitated, by hissing, while males make a more manly, harsh croaking sound.

Fulmars and Foul Smells

Don't try to get too close to the fulmars though. They have a nasty habit of squirting unwelcome visitors with a particularly foul-smelling fishy oil, regurgitated from their stomachs. They use this defensive weapon on other birds that come too close to their nests, as well as on humans. The smell of the oil is a stink that defeats even the best of detergents when you try to shift it from your clothes. The fulmar is a skilled airman, feathered in silver-grey and white, and has prominent nostrils on top of its beak. To the unskilled eye, it is superficially similar to the silver-grey and white herring gull, but watch them flying, and you should soon see how the fulmar glides with its wings rigid, much more often than the herring gulls do. You will find most of the fulmars on the May nest on the cliffs along the south-west side of the island.

Fulmar

Auks and Others

Among the other cliff-nesting birds to be seen are the herring gulls, of course, and kittiwakes, guillemots and razorbills. Of these, the guillemots are sharp-eyed, sharp-beaked birds, resplendent in white, but with dark brown feathers around the head. They tend to nest on fairly broad ledges of the cliffs, generally in pretty inaccessible places. Young guillemots are given a harsh introduction to the joys of flying and swimming. They generally get encouraged by their parents to launch themselves off the cliff ledges while they are still tiny, and only about three weeks after hatching. Immature wings all a-flutter, they fall erratically down for maybe 40 metres (120 feet or so) and splash into the waves, where they seem immediately to feel at home, diving and swimming like little experts. Guillemots fly low over the water, with a whirring wing movement, often with their legs outstretched and trailing behind their tail.

Razorbills are handsome birds, easily recognisable from their heavy, powerful-looking bills. They have a clear white line running from under their eyes to the bill, and another almost vertical stripe on the bill. If you spot one with its beak open, you will be surprised at the brilliance of the yellow colour inside the bird's bill and throat. Their lower plumage is white, while the upper feathers are black, with a neat white strip edging the wings. In contrast to the guillemots, the razorbills tend to pick narrower ledges and crannies in the cliffs to nest, and rear their chicks in. Both in flight and on the water, they very closely resemble their cousins the guillemots.

Though it otherwise resembles the razorbill, the guillemot has a sharply pointed beak

If you are not a bird expert, you could be excused if you were to become somewhat confused, on hearing bird watchers referring to the auks they have seen on the Isle of May. There is a handsome little black and white bird known as the little auk, and you can quite frequently see some of these, usually a little out to sea, off the Isle of May. But the guillemot, puffin and the razorbill are all also members of the Auk (or *Alcidae*) family, and are quite often referred to generically simply as "auks" by ornithologists.

Terns and Kittiwakes

Tern

The terns have a very different habitat on the May from the various auks. Instead of nesting on cliffs, they make their nests in loose sandy soil around the higher parts of the island, close to the lighthouse and on the North plateau. They are mid-grey above and almost white grey below. Their wingtips are dark and their heads are black. In the air they display a forked tail and move in a lightly undulating flight path, with a regular measured wing beat. Their usual calls in flight are also quite distinctive, a sort of "kik-kik-kik" sound plus an occasional "Keerree". Amateur bird watchers needn't really try to pick out the various types of tern. All tend to breed in the same areas, and spotting the rather minor differences between the Arctic, common, Sandwich and roseate terns is something probably best left to the experts.

You should, however, be able to tell the kittiwakes apart from the other birds of the Isle of May, without too much difficulty. They are rather delicate little birds, with sharply defined black wingtips. They tend to fly in a smoother,

Kittiwake

more buoyant manner than herring gulls, but if your eyes won't distinguish the kittiwake for you, your ears should help. Their typical cry around the breeding colonies is a deafening "kitt-ee-wayke" interrupted at times by a low "uk-uk-uk" and occasionally you might hear one make a sound that is uncannily like the crying of a human baby.

Ducks

The eiders are easiest of all to tell apart form the other birds that breed in the Isle of May. They nest all over the place, and sometimes in the most unlikely situations. You can find them hidden in vegetation, or nestled close to a rock for shelter. If you do happen to disturb a nest with a clutch of eggs, do try to cover the eggs again with camouflaging down, as the ducks do, to keep them out of sight of the gulls. Otherwise, instead of hatching into ducklings, these eggs are liable to become some hungry gull's supper. Most of the eiders are to found on the north-east side of the May, close to the shoreline, and many seem relatively unperturbed by the presence of human visitors. The females are rather nondescript speckled browny creatures, but the drake is very smartly turned out in white, with black markings on top of his head, tail, wingtips and underparts, and with a distinct green to the side of his neck. Unfortunately, when he is moulting, the drake can become any sort of jumble between mottled brown and this full multicolour uniform.

Bird Traps

In addition to these types which breed on the May, the island plays host to hundreds of other species flying in and out, in the course of their migrationary journeys. Sometimes the whole island is carpeted with these visitors, searching for rest, food and shelter wherever it is to be found, while overhead thousands more fill the air, as they head for landfall elsewhere. It is in the spring and in September and October each year that observers see the greatest numbers of migrant visitors on the May. You may come across some examples of what are known as a Heligoland Trap on the island. These consist of cunning funnels of wire mesh, tapering into a catching box, and are used by ornithologists to catch some of these migratory birds. The name of the traps comes from the German island, where such traps first were put into service. The aim of trapping is to ring the birds, so identifying them as having been visitors to the May, and enabling research to be done, in conjunction with ornithologists elsewhere in the world, on whence these birds have come from, and where they are heading for, after leaving the Isle of May. The birds are not harmed in any way.

There is little point in trying to make a comprehensive list here of even the more common of the migratory birds that have been observed on the Isle of May. Specialist books, and the log books in the May's Bird Observatory do this already, for enthusiasts, and this book is written more for the generally interested visitor, rather than for the expert. Suffice it to say that any visitor, at the right times of year, can look forward to spotting regular visitors such as goldcrests, robins, skylarks, buntings, shrikes, chiff-chaffs, skuas, petrels, gannets, little auks, snipe, warblers of various types, flycatchers, shearwaters, fieldfares, redstarts, plovers, cuckoos, owls and various species of ducks and geese. Keen ornithologists can make exciting new sightings here, especially when the weather systems are so configured as to drive migrant birds out of their usual routes. In autumn, there are frequently vast numbers of relatively common birds. There is only a limited area of island for the visitors to settle, and only limited cover where they can hide. As a result, many of the rarer species are more easily seen here by expert eyes, than almost anywhere on mainland Britain.

Serious bird watchers can arrange to spend long periods observing the bird life on the May. The Northern Lighthouse Board for many years made available to them the old Low Light building (see Chapter 6) as their headquarters. Observers based there maintain a daily census of birds, write descriptions of rare visitors, keep a log-book detailing migrations and constantly up-date a diary of their day to day activities. This light-hearted diary is often eagerly read by their successor occupants of the Low Light. The accommodation comprises a living room, a bedroom with four beds, a washroom, and outside toilet and a kitchen. It isn't quite the Ritz Hotel, but then, anything like the Ritz would be totally out of keeping with the spartan surroundings of the Isle of May.

This Chapter is by no means a recognition guide to all the birds you may see on a visit to the Isle of May. It was never intended to be. It probably hasn't even helped the average visitor all that much, to pick out the difference between a shag and a seagull. But never mind. You can still at least enjoy the sight and the sound (and the smell) of these many thousands of birds that wheel through the skies above and around the Island, providing us with a fascinating scene of constant aerial activity.

Metal Birds

Mention of all this aerial activity takes me briefly to the aircraft that fly in the vicinity of the Isle of May. Despite the fact that the Island is a National Nature Reserve, the air space around and above it is not subject to any special restrictions, so far as aircraft movements are concerned. One of the Royal Air Force's major jet fighter bases is at Leuchars, just 15 miles away to the north-west of the Isle of May. Although there are no navigation radio aids for aircraft on the May, the island is still an outstanding visual landmark from the air. As a result, pilots of Tornados and other aircraft approaching Leuchars from the south frequently make use of the island as a turning point when they are flying in towards this busy RAF base. The sudden roar of these low-flying jets normally doesn't seem to disturb the birds unduly, which is more than you can say for some of the humans on the island at the time.

From time to time, civilian light aircraft also overfly the May on sight-seeing or photographic flights, but there is no landing strip for a fixed-wing aircraft, anywhere on the island. There is a helicopter landing pad, a little to the north of Kirkhaven, but this is normally used only by flights directly connected with Scottish Natural Heritage work, bringing in supplies or construction materials. It is also available for emergency evacuation of sick people.

Chapter 5
Other Wildlife of the Island

In contrast to the bewildering variety of bird life that is to be seen on the Isle of May, its range of animal life is rather more limited.

Land Creatures

By far the most obvious species on land here is the rabbit. There are rabbit burrows all over the place, assiduously dug by these beasts. They are probably the descendants of the rabbits first introduced to the May, back around the year 1330, by the monks, who used them as a source of food and revenue. The number of rabbits on the island has gone up and down like a yo-yo, over the years, as diseases and shortages of food take their toll. Then the surviving rabbits, finding more food available for the smaller numbers that are left, start raising larger families again, and another population explosion occurs. The island seems to be able to support a maximum of approximately 2,000 rabbits. Some competition for burrows continually takes place between the rabbits and the puffins during the puffin breeding season. Between them, the rabbits and the puffins are responsible for quite a lot of erosion of the island's rather limited amount of fertile soil.

House-mice also inhabit the island in large numbers, up to around 6,000 of them , according to some estimates. They seem to be slightly larger than their mainland cousins, and make good eating for the owls and kestrels that regularly feed on them. It seems strange, considering the number of ships that have been wrecked near the Isle of May, that no rats have ever colonised the island. In view of the havoc that rats can wreak on bird populations, by destroying nests and devouring both eggs and young, it is certainly a blessing that this is the case.

Although for much of the past three centuries, sheep have been kept on the island (over 50 of them in the early 1960s) there currently are none. The only other creatures (man excepted) that you are now likely to come across in any numbers on the land surface of the Isle of May are ants, and the large common snail. When it is wet, these snails come out in such large numbers that in some parts of the island it is hard to walk without crunching some of their shells underfoot. These snails form one of the links in the food chain, especially for the oystercatchers, and some of the land birds that occasionally breed on the island.

Bats and Butterflies

Quite frequently, the island gets visited by bats. These are usually pipistrelles, but the long-eared bat has also been seen. There are often lots of butterflies too. The small tortoiseshell is the most common of these, often seen making good use of the island's large thistle crop, for nectar supplies. These hibernate in various places on the island, but many other species of butterfly arrive from time to time on the island, as migrants. These include the painted lady, small copper, small white and large white. Migrating moths are also seen, often fluttering around the lighted windows of the observatory in the Low Light building.

In contrast to the rather limited range of animal life above the high water mark on the Isle of May, it is a different story from that mark, down towards low water mark and into the sea. This teems with many different forms of life.

Creatures of the Shoreline

The rock pools are full of small fish, shrimp, shanny, water fleas, sea anemones, limpets, mussels, hermit crabs, shore crabs, starfish and, of course, seaweeds. Over sixty different varieties of seaweed have been recorded, growing around the shores of the May.

On the two small stretches of sandy beach, at Silver Sands and Kirkhaven, you can find many different types of sea shells, and occasionally you may be lucky enough to come on a sea urchin. You will of course, also come across all manner of jetsam, the junk and debris cast on shore from the sea. Much of this consists of plastic, a material that unfortunately does not naturally decompose in sea water, and does not improve the attractiveness of the coastline. Some must originate from the mainland farther up the Firth, but a great deal seems to have been thoughtlessly jettisoned overboard from boats and ships.

Fishermen from Anstruther and Cellardyke set lines of lobster pots off the May, to catch partans (edible crabs) and lobsters, and specimens of these creatures sometimes are washed up along the shores of the island. Observant visitors to the Isle of May can often see pods of bottlenose dolphins looping and diving their way past the island. There are sometimes also common porpoises to be seen and on, rare occasions, orca and minke whales have also been sighted in the waters around the May. However, the sea mammals that capture the attention of most visitors are, of course, the seals.

Seals

The Isle of May is one of just three breeding grounds (known as "rookeries") along the east coast of Britain of the Atlantic seal, otherwise called the grey seal. The other two are on the Farne Islands, off the Northumberland coast, and on Scroby Sands, in Norfolk. Grey seals have been long-time inhabitants of the Isle of May.

Young grey seal pup

One record, dated 1508, shows that the hermit of the May was paid 13 shillings for a seal he brought to King James IV. These grey seals are occasionally joined on the May for a while, by harbour seals (formerly known as common seals) although the harbour seal is more a creature of sandy beaches and sandbanks, such as those in and around the Firth of Tay. The harbour seals that visit the May most probably come from that area of the coast, although seals can, and do, cover remarkable distances at sea.

The grey seal population of the May fluctuates considerably. It increased greatly during the late 1970s when steps were taken to reduce the number of seals in the Farne Islands. Finding themselves unwelcome there (they were destroying puffin breeding grounds) many of the Farne Island seals found their way to the Isle of May, and settled down here. Each year the number of grey seals on the Isle of May seems to rise from just a little over a hundred in spring and early summer, to many times that number by the autumn, when the first of the seal pups are born. As October moves into November and then December, more and more new seal pups arrive, are suckled by their mothers for about three weeks, then start to explore the shore and the rock pools on their own.

Baby seals have beautiful big saucer eyes, and a light-coloured furry puppy coat. They spend a lot of time lolling around and sleeping, and can make the most plaintive crying and groaning noises. But, attractive as they may look, they also have teeth, are not very fond of humans coming too close, and are not in the least averse to biting, quite viciously. Their parents, especially the cows, can be quite protective of their families too. They are able to muster up a surprising speed on dry land for such ponderous looking creatures, and will not hesitate to charge towards any human being that they see as being a menace to their pups.

Bull grey seals are larger than their mates, their heads are less sleek, and their necks are thicker and more deeply corrugated. They are territorial animals, each having a harem of five to a dozen cows, which they will defend with noisy growls and threatening movements, if any other bull seal comes near. The cows also attack the bulls, and bite their necks at times, whenever they think the bulls are lumbering too close to their pups. In contrast to their clumsy appearance on land, and their general awkwardness out of the water, seals are marvellous swimmers. They cannot breath under water, but seem to be capable of staying below the surface for up to about

20 minutes at a time, sometimes covering long distances as they do so. They can sleep in the water, either taking naps for up to 20 minutes before coming up for air, or at times snoozing vertically, with their noses just out of the water to let them

Grey seal pup   breath. This is known as "bottling".

Vegetation, Wild Flowers and Weeds

The plant life on the island is quite varied too. When I made my first visit to the May, in the 1950s, I don't think there was a single tree growing on the Island, but there now are several managing to cling to a precarious existence, despite the salt spray, almost constant wind, and regular winter gales. A few trees have been planted around the Heligoland traps (see Chapter 4) to attract birds to the traps. These also incidentally provide some cover for some of the migrant birds. These are sycamores, sitka spruce, elder and willow, which need the protection of walls to survive.

One field, between Kirkhaven Jetty and the Chapel, is well-named Thistle Field, and can present a wonderful display of purple thistle heads. It has presumably been like this for centuries, but other parts of the island have changed their flora quite significantly with the passing of the years. The colonies of gulls have far reaching effects of plant life, and on Rona, one area that used to be thick with thrift flowers about twenty years ago, is now a mass of chickweed, sea campion and sorrel. Luckily, thrift, with its purply pink flowers does still flourish elsewhere on the island, and makes a lovely sight when in bloom. In summer, large areas of the island turn white with the flowers of the sea campion. You can find Lesser Celandines in sheltered spots, and violets grow in profusion on the sides of Holyman's Road and the Low Road. Elsewhere, buttercups, daisies, wood burdock, dandelion, lovage, silverweed, sea wormwood, English stonecrop, and even marsh orchids can be found.

The Isle of May is the proud possessor of at least one species of plant life that does not seem to grow anywhere else on the mainland. This, the only plant said to be peculiar to the island is known as the Least Water Parsnip, a plant of the parsley family which has the botanical name of *Heliosciadium Innudatum.*

There is a huge heap of ash on the island, near the beacon (for the origin of this unusual feature, have a look in Chapter 6) and this has generated a selection of wild flowers, including nettles, burdock, creeping buttercup, thistles and forget-me-nots. The ashy area has recently also become the home of rather a nasty poisonous weed, henbane. This has hairy, sticky stems that grow to about a metre in height, with jagged leaves, and virulent yellow, purple-veined flowers that turn to seeds in the autumn. It also has an unpleasant smell, and is best left strictly alone. There are many other, more attractive and more interesting plants and flowers for visitors to the Isle of May to enjoy.

Chapter 6
The Story of the Lighthouses

The Firth of Forth has been an important arm of the sea for Scottish maritime commerce, ever since records began. And the Isle of May, situated as it is across an otherwise clear and safe channel for shipping, has, over the years, taken a toll of many vessels that have been wrecked around its jagged rocky coastline.

While the island belonged to Alexander Cunnynghame (see Chapter 3), he began to make plans to erect some sort of beacon on the island, to warn passing ships about the dangerous rocks there. It was probably a petition drawn up by a Kilrenny man, Alexander Beaton, and his fellow skippers, to have some form of light on the May, that inspired Cunnynghame to proceed with the work. Not everyone was in favour of the idea, though. Some believed that a lighthouse was a form of religious defiance, others that there was no need for one, and still others never believed one would work at all. One skipper, John Cowtrey from Largs, stated that a light on the May would simply lead to ships being destroyed on the Carr Rocks off the Firth of Tay. Another, James Lochoir of Kinghorn, expressed his belief that captains of ships that ran aground on the May were just idiots, and that no lighthouse there could save them from their own stupidity. Locals living along the Fife coast were not all in favour either. The cargo from wrecked ships, and the fabric of the ships themselves, were regarded by many as part of their rightful livelihood. Flotsam, jetsam, wreck and plunder often made a valuable contribution to a meagre level of existence.

Scotland's First Lighthouse

Despite all these complaints and opposition, Cunnynghame persisted with his idea of a light on the May. His first attempt took the form of a stubby tower with a platform about 12 metres (40 feet) in height, with a burning beacon on top. This began to function in 1636, and was the first and only lighthouse of any type around the coasts of Scotland, although several were already in use by this time, around the English coast. The cost of building and running the beacon were defrayed by the levying of an unofficial impost on all the ships that passed the Isle of May.

It fell to his Alexander's son, John Cunnynghame, to achieve some improvements on this first product of his father's bright idea. It was a certain Thomas Bikkertoun who made this financially possible for John Cunnynghame, by arranging that mariners could have the benefit of a better beacon, provided they were prepared to pay an official toll, based on the tonnage of their ships. Bikkertoun asked Parliament that these dues should be similar to the tolls being charged for the use of the lights

Reconstruction drawing showing the 17th century beacon on the Isle of May, its chauffer blazing, and piles of cinders and ash around its base.
(Illustration reproduced by permission of the Archaeological Unit of Fife Council Planning Service)

already installed at places on the English coast. It was eventually agreed to levy a fee of two shillings (Scots) per ton for all Scottish ships and four shillings (Scots) per ton for all foreign (including English) vessels. Every ship entering Scottish waters between Dunottar and St Abbs Head was liable for this toll. The arrangements for collecting the monies were made through Customs officers at each of the Scottish ports around the Firth of Forth.

The legal document that allowed collection of this official toll (known as the Patent), was granted by the Scottish Parliament in 1645 to John Cunnynghame together with James Maxwell. To improve the light from the beacon, and so justify the charges, they set about building an extension to the original platform. They built up the tower, making it look rather like a Border keep, to a height of 18 metres (60 feet), half as high again as the original light. This was completed in 1656. At the top of the tower, surrounded by a parapet, they installed what was called a "chauffer", a sort of metal brazier in which coal was burned to produce the light. This system consumed an average of around one ton of coal each night; less in the short summer nights, but considerably more when the fire had to burn throughout the longer winter hours of darkness. When the wind rose to around gale force, more than three tons could go up in flames in a single winter night.

Every few days a fresh supply of coal had to be shipped across from Fife to the May, where it was dumped in the shallow water at Kirkhaven. From there, the solitary lighthouse keeper had to pick it out of the water and carry it on his back up from Kirkhaven to the beacon. This had, of course, been built on the highest point of the Island. There, the coal had to be hoisted vertically, using a rope and bucket on a simple derrick, 18 metres up to the top platform. The fuel supply had to be constant, so the chauffer could give out its continuous warning light. It was not until the poor man had kept the fire alight for several years, more or less constantly (at a salary of £7 per annum plus 30 bushels of meal for his family) that someone took pity on him and provided him with an assistant keeper and a horse.

To pay for the upkeep of the beacon, and for the 300 to 400 tons of coal it consumed each year, the income from the shipping tolls initially amounted to around £280 sterling per annum. Coal must have been less expensive in the 17th century than it is now! Admittedly, that £280 is reckoned to be equivalent to something between £80,000 and £100,000 in present day money. By 1790, the annual tolls had risen to £960, and just ten years later, in 1800, this had become £1,500, largely as a result of increases in the tonnage of shipping passing the Isle of May.

Witchcraft

One sad incident occurred during the construction of John Cunnynghame's light on the May. This was when the architect of the tower, while returning from a visit to the Isle of May to supervise the work, was drowned. His boat capsized in sudden Forth squall, between the Isle of May and Pittenweem. It seems that, even by this time, not everyone in the east Neuk was in favour of having a lighthouse on the May, and stories grew that some would-be ship wreckers, whose aims were being thwarted by the light, had engaged witchcraft, to help them in their evil trade. Several old ladies from East Neuk villages, including one Eppie Laing from Anstruther, were accused of having used witchcraft to call up the sudden squall that killed the architect. As was then the custom (following the drawing up, in 1643, of the Presbyterian Church's Solemn League and Covenant), these poor women were tried by the local clergy. They were, as almost always happened, found guilty of the crime, and put to death by burning at the stake. This hideous punishment was quite a common occurrence around the East Neuk in these days. Local parish records for 1643 and 1644 still proudly show a list of over thirty unfortunate women, who were given this "faggot and stake" treatment within a few months, for various alleged crimes of witchcraft, adultery with warlocks, and suchlike wickedness.

The coal-burning brazier on the May was eventually manned by three attendants, two of whom were on constant watch each night. The fire needed stoking every half hour, or even more frequently in high winds. It was never entirely satisfactory, for various reasons, but it continued to give service to sailors for over 150 years. The main problem with the system was that, in high winds, very little light could be seen by seamen who were viewing it from the windward, which was, of course, the dangerous side of the island. This was because the keepers couldn't light that side on rough nights, as they had to use the iron bars there to steady themselves against the gale, while stoking the other side. But the coal light was better than no light at all, so it was kept burning on and on, year after year.

Seven Deaths in One Night

One night, in January 1791, the light went out, and remained out for two nights, during a severe storm. When sailors eventually managed to land on the island to find out what had happened, they discovered the lighthouse keeper, George Anderson, his wife and five of their six children dead or dying in their beds. One baby survived. The calamity had been caused when sparks from the blazing light had fallen onto the piles of ash that lay around the tower. These had then started to smoulder, fanned by the gale. The ashes gave off poisonous sulphur dioxide and carbon monoxide gas, which seeped inside the Anderson family sleeping quarters in the beacon, and asphyxiated them, while they slept.

Despite this tragic event, the coal-burning light on the May continued to be used for another twenty years. Many of the ships entering and leaving the Forth were greatly helped by the it, but its uncertainty was the cause of several shipwrecks over the years. Complaints about it from fishermen and other mariners continued to grow, but nothing was done until, in 1810, the Royal Navy lost two of its ships. The gun frigates *Pallas* and *Nymph* were on their way from Norway to Leith when they were both wrecked on rocks near Dunbar. It was alleged that their navigators had mistaken the flames from a limekiln on the Lothian coast for the smoky old May light, and had taken the actual the May light to be the Bell Rock. Following this, the Government was forced to act, and it was decided to replace the ancient brazier on the May, with the latest design of efficient oil lamps and reflectors.

The Main Light or Tower

As mentioned in Chapter 3, the Commissioners of Northern Lights purchased the Isle of May in 1815. They engaged Robert Stevenson (the uncle of writer Robert Louis Stevenson) to build the replacement light. Robert Stevenson had only recently spent four years working on the construction of the Bell Rock Light, out in the North Sea, 19 km (12 miles) south-east of Arbroath. This was completed in 1811, and enhanced his already excellent reputation as a lighthouse engineer. Stevenson's design for the Isle of May turned out to be the impressive large building with its sturdy square central tower which has, ever since its completion, been the most prominent feature of the Isle of May.

The stonemasons prepared the masonry for the new buildings in the same yard in Arbroath as Stevenson had used when building the Bell Rock light. The quarry blocks were shipped to Arbroath harbour, transported to the Bell Rock Yard where they were dressed to shape, then returned to the harbour for shipment to the Isle of May. Builders based on the island used these to construct the handsome building that can still be seen dominating the skyline of the Isle of May. Its architectural style of Castellated Tudor Gothic, crowned by an elegantly domed glazed cage for the light, may not harmonise very well with its surroundings, (it has scornfully been called Stevenson's "Toy Fort") but its structure has certainly stood the test of time. Inside, the building still shows that money seems to have been no object during its construction. Solid wood internal doors in the tower are crafted into curves that blend perfectly with the curvature of the walls. Lighthouse keepers' quarters have handsome marble mantlepieces around their fireplaces, some complete with beautifully carved relief designs.

The construction of the new lighthouse was completed in January 1816, and the last coal fire in the chauffer of the old Beacon was allowed to flicker out, just as dawn broke on 1 February 1816. That was almost exactly 180 years since the first fire had been kindled in the first May Beacon. The ash that remained from the more than 60,000 tons of coal that must have been burned over these years, was simply dumped around the base of the Beacon, and much of it is still there, overgrown, and forming a soil that seems to suit the poisonous weed henbane which, as mentioned in Chapter 5, now grows prolifically around the old Beacon tower.

The oil lamps of the new lighthouse went into service at dusk on 1st February 1816, their reliable bright beam giving a much improved guide for seafarers. The new light is over 24 metres (80 feet) high, and stands on the highest point of the island, nearly 50 metres (160 feet) above mean sea level. The light is thus about 74 metres (240 feet) above sea level, and the sequence of four rapid flashes of the original oil light could be seen from ships up to 34 kilometres (21 miles) away. The old beacon tower was, unfortunately, too tall. It formed a blind spot, or cast a shadow behind which seamen could not see the new light. Stevenson therefore decided to demolish it.

By coincidence, the writer, Sir Walter Scott had decided to visit the May to see the new light and while there managed to persuade Robert Stevenson not to totally destroy this historic old building, the first lighthouse ever to have been built in Scotland. Scott suggested it be "ruined *a la picturesque*" instead. Stevenson therefore only reduced it in height sufficiently to ensure the new light could be seen from all directions. The lower part of the beacon, with a pitched roof, which Stevenson added over its ground floor vault, still stands. This is the whitewashed square building that can be seen just a few paces east of the new lighthouse. It was scheduled as an Ancient Monument in 1958, and is now approaching its 400th birthday.

Improvements to the Light

The new Stevenson lighthouse functioned unaltered until 1843, when the 27-year old oil lamps were replaced by a new dioptric lamp system, still oil-lit. This was the brain-child of Sir David Brewster, who was principle of St Salvator and St Leonards at St Andrews University, and had also, in 1816, invented the kaleidoscope.

The following year, 1844, saw the construction of the Low Light on the north-east coast of the Island. This has a round tower with a corbelled parapet and a domed lantern, with accommodation for the lighthouse keeper alongside. These are the buildings now used by ornithologists as a bird observatory. The idea behind building

The reservoir tanks and pipelines that formerly supplied air to the foghorns can still be seen across Fluke Street from the compressor house. Palpitation Brae leads up from here to the main Tower lighthouse.

the Low Light was to enable seafarers leaving the Tay Estuary to navigate past the dangerous North Carr Rocks, off Fife Ness. By sighting the position of the steady beam from the Low Light against the intermittent flashes from the main Isle of May lighthouse, the sailors could adjust their course to keep clear of the Carr Rocks. The system worked reasonably well for about fifty years, but the Low Light became redundant when the North Carr Lightship was stationed just off the Carr Rocks around the start of the 20th century.

In 1885, a major change took place. The oil lamps were superseded by electric lights. The Isle of May lighthouse became the first in Scotland to use electricity. The power for the lights was generated on the island by a steam-powered dynamo. To house the increased numbers of personnel now required to maintain the light, the rather plain block of keepers' houses and machinery buildings in Fluke Street, to the south of the lighthouse, were also built in 1885. The Isle of May now had a single, revolving, group-flashing electric light.

The number of keepers and other personnel has dwindled steadily over the last 100 years. Changes in technology enabled the large number of men involved to be reduced in 1924. This was done by introducing a single incandescent mantle, lit by burning vapourised oil, which had its beam magnified by a system of lenses. This light still gave a double flash every 20 seconds, and was visible over the same 34 km (21 mile) distance as was the original 1816 fixed oil lamp. When the Low Light was switched off, its keepers left. The technical improvements of 1924 led to other departures. The replacement of steam by diesel power for the dynamos cut numbers again. In the years immediately following WW2, four keepers and their families manned the light, the generators, and the fog horns that had been installed to boom out audible warnings over the sea from both North and South Ness. In 1972, the Isle of May was deemed to be a "rock station" and as a consequence, keepers' families were no longer permitted to stay on the island. The four keepers continued to be relieved at monthly intervals until, on 13 March 1989, the light became fully automated. When the last keeper left the Isle of May, his departure ended a tradition that had lasted for over three and a half centuries.

As folk singer and song writer Nick Keir put it in part of his song *Keepers* (recorded on the CD *Keepers* CDTRAX 174 by the McCalmans

Proud men they were who manned the beacon,
A sense of worth was in their mind.
Maybe they're on shore now, aye, but still on look-out
As the doors rattle in an unsensed wind.

The empty room, the untrod stairway,
The only sound the roaring sea.
The tables and the chairs wait for one last supper
As the mist closes in unseen.

Ardnamurchan, Loch Indaal, Rattray Head, The Isle of May,
Not an eye to watch the sea, from Eilann Glas or Copinsay,
Still they guard the shore,
Fair Isle North and Skerryvore.

How the Lighthouse Works in 2000

Since 1989 the light has been switched on and off by a photo-electric cell which senses the change of light intensity at dusk and dawn. The light now comprises two banks of low voltage electric lamps, similar to automotive headlamps, mounted on a rotating turntable base. The power is direct current electricity, supplied from banks of lead-acid accumulators or batteries in the ground floor of the Tower. These are kept charged by diesel-powered alternators. The turntable is also powered by these batteries and its speed of rotation, together with the fixed angle between the two sets of lights, determines the intervals between the flashes that identify the Isle of May light. The correct operation of the system is constantly monitored via signals to Fife Ness, by the Commissioners of Northern Lights in Edinburgh.

Improved navigation equipment, radar, echo-sounders and Global Positioning Systems (GPS) on most vessels, large and small, that pass near the May, have now rendered the fog horns redundant. The compressors, pressure vessels and long pipelines leading to the North and South horn are gradually decaying in the salty air. Who knows, it may not be much longer before even the steady flashing of the light on the Isle of May is considered to be unnecessary for safe navigation? If and when the light is finally switched off, the wheel will have turned full circle since Alexander Cunnynghame installed Scotland's first-ever lighthouse here, in 1636.

The three lighthouses of the Isle of May. The truncated
17th century beacon, on the left; the 1816 main light or
Tower, centre; and the 1844 Low Light, lower right. Only
the Tower still operates as a lighthouse.

Chapter 7
Wars and the May

Considering its strategic position, guarding the mouth of the Firth that leads inland towards Scotland's capital city, it is not surprising that the Isle of May has had its part to play in several military and naval campaigns and wars.

Viking Murders

The first recorded fighting on or near the May occurred in 875, when Danish Vikings, aided and abetted by the Picts, were waging war on the Scots. The Vikings won a one-sided victory over St Adrian and his peace-loving monks who, as described in Chapter 3, were at that time taking refuge at their monastery on the island. There may have been warlike acts between earlier settlers on the island (some graves on the May have been carbon-dated as the 5th century AD) and other invaders from the sea, but if there were, no evidence of this remains today.

Anglo-Scottish Conflict

The next recorded episode of conflict concerning the Isle of May was between the Scots and the English. King David I of Scotland (1124-53), who had King Henry I of England as a brother-in-law, built a chapel dedicated the St Adrian on the island and then presented the whole Isle of May to the Benedictine Monastery of Reading, in England. In exchange he was promised the services of nine priests in perpetuity, to say Mass for his soul and those of his successors, in St Adrian's Chapel. The May remained under English control for about 120 years, until King Alexander III of Scotland (1241-86) decided he disliked the presence of a foreign-controlled island in the Firth of Forth. He persuaded William Wishart, the Archbishop of St Andrews, to buy back the May from the Abbot of Reading, and this transaction took place, in some secrecy, about 1270. Once news of the deal leaked out the English did their best to rescind it, but in vain.

After Alexander III was thrown from his horse and killed, near Kinghorn in Fife, and then his daughter the Maid of Norway died in 1290, Edward I of England installed John de Baliol (nicknamed the "Toom Tabard" by the Scots) on the vacant throne of his "vassal kingdom" of Scotland in 1292. Baliol's very first Parliament was asked to return the Isle of May to the Benedictine monks of Reading. Wishart's successor, Bishop Fraser of St Andrews delayed any settlement, first by arguing about repayment of the money paid to Reading Monastery, then by appealing to Pope Nicholas IV for a ruling. It is probable that, after the English defeated the Scots at the Battle of

Dunbar in 1296, the May did return to the control of Reading, but the matter of which nation ruled the May was finally settled when Scotland gained her independence after the Battle of Bannockburn in 1314.

The English did not accept this state of affairs quietly. From time to time throughout the 14th and 15th centuries, their navy made attacks and incursions on the Isle of May. They repeatedly laid waste the land that was being cultivated by the monks and they stripped the Priory of all its remaining treasures. They then despoiled, and in the end virtually flattened, all the Priory buildings on the Isle of May. At this time, St Adrian's Priory had been one of Scotland's wealthiest religious establishments. Thereafter, for some two-hundred years, every time the Scots built anything of value on the May, the English navy sailed in and smashed it up again.

Naval Battles

However, they didn't always have things all their own way. 15th century Scotland was also a naval force to be reckoned with, and in the reign of King James IV there were several violent naval encounters close to the Isle of May. In 1488, for instance, Andrew Wood of Largo, a Scottish naval commander, set sail in his two vessels the *Yellow Carvel* and the *Flower* to attack an English naval force of five ships that was had entered the Firth of Forth and was attempting to pillage Scottish harbours. He triumphantly captured all five ships of the English fleet, and brought them in to Leith as trophies of war.

When the English King Henry VII heard of this, he was furious, and ordered the English admiral Sir Stephen Bull to bring Andrew Wood to London, dead or alive. Bull learned of an expedition that a ship captained by Andrew Wood was making to Flanders in 1490. He hatched a plan to lay an ambush to attack Wood as he returned to Scotland. He waited at anchor, hidden in the lee of the Isle of May, with three English Navy vessels, well armed with troops and artillery. Bull also made use of a captured fishing vessel, pressed into service as a look-out scout. And on Wood's approach the superior English force pounced upon the Scots ships.

The battle commenced early in the morning, just off the Isle of May. It raged all day. Cannons were fired; archers let fly storms of arrows from their crossbows; lime pots and fireballs were hoisted aloft; grappling irons called into service; there was man-to-man combat, with spears and two-handed swords. Darkness finally brought respite to the exhausted and tattered crews of both sides, but at dawn, battle was resumed. The ships gradually ran north, towards the Firth of Tay, where crowds came out to line the banks and cheer the Scots to victory. Sir Stephen Bull's fleet finally ran aground on sandbanks at the mouth of the Tay, and all the English ships were captured and brought in by Andrew Wood to Dundee.

King James later decided to send the three ships back to England together with all the Englishmen taken prisoner by Wood, as a gesture of goodwill to them, as "the stout and hardy warriors" they had proved to be. With them went a message from

King James to King Henry. This stated that James "therefore desired him to send no more captains in time coming" for he had proved there were better seamen than these, already in Scotland.

Andrew Wood was knighted for his gallantry in these engagements, and granted grounds in Largo, Fife. In 1491 the King appointed Sir Andrew Wood as his pilot to the Isle of May, in the following terms: "...being skilful in pyloting, he should be ready, upon the King's call, to pylot and convey him and the Queen in visit to St Adrian's Chapel."

Sir Andrew Wood was again sailing just off the May in 1512, on the maiden voyage of a fine new vessel. Now he was commander of King James IV's huge new warship *The Great Michael*, the flagship of Scotland's new navy. *The Great Michael* had taken six years (1506-12) to construct and fit out at Newhaven, near Edinburgh. To provide enough timber to build it, most of Fife, except around the royal palace at Falkland, had been denuded of trees. After James IV's death at Flodden, *the Great Michael* was sold to the French Navy, and ended its days sadly as a rotting hulk in Dieppe.

The Spanish Armada

In 1588 another ship manned by naval seamen passed close to the Isle of May, heading towards Anstruther. This time the crew was Spanish rather than English, although the vessel itself was Scottish. It was crewed by survivors of the famous Spanish Armada, which the English claim was defeated by Sir Francis Drake in the Channel, which the Dutch claim was defeated by their Navy in the North Sea off Scheveningen, but which in fact probably owed its failure more to bad weather than to the prowess of either of its enemy navies. The ship that passed the Isle of May carried 260 hungry men under the command of Don Jan de Gomez de Medina. He had been commander of a squadron of twenty galleons, most of which had been wrecked on Fair Isle, and he was coming to Anstruther in a ship acquired in the Northern Isles, looking for help from the Scots to get back to Spain. He was soon provided with the much needed food and assistance.

Scotland at that time was not feeling at all friendly towards England and its Queen Elizabeth, who had just executed Mary Queen of Scots. Many Scots, including the good folk of Anstruther, were quite prepared to help any enemy of the English. The Spanish crewmen were given temporary accommodation by the people of Anstruther while their ship was readied to sail again. In much finer fettle, they soon sailed back past the Isle of May again on course for Spain. By coincidence, on his way home, Jan de Gomez came across an Anstruther ship that was under arrest in the French port of Calais. He told the authorities about Anstruther's generosity toward his crew, and arranged for the Scottish ship's release. Before the two ships sailed from Calais, the Spaniards southward and the Scots towards the north, this true Spanish gentleman asked the Scottish crew to convey his grateful compliments to the minister of Anstruther and to the good people of the town.

The Jacobite Risings

The next war to involve the Isle of May was the Jacobite Rising of 1715. The "Old Pretender", James Francis Edward Stuart, who landed at Peterhead in December 1715, raised an army of Highlanders to fight for him in his attempt to claim the throne of Scotland. A force of his men, led by Mackintosh of Borlum, took over the East Neuk villages in Fife, and there proclaimed him as "King James the Eighth". He is said to have been lying at anchor at this time, in the shelter of the Isle of May. But English ships arrived to patrol the Firth of Forth, trying to prevent the Jacobites penetrating any farther south. Mackintosh of Borlum sent some of his Jacobites to make a diversionary manoeuvre at Burntisland, to draw off the Hanoverian navy, while the main force, under Lord Strathmore, sailed from Crail, Anstruther and St Monance towards North Berwick on the Lothian coast.

About a thousand men got across, before the Royal Navy returned from Burntisland, and fell upon the next flotilla of small boats full of Jacobite soldiers. Many of the Jacobites did still manage across to North Berwick, but some were captured by the English ships, and about three hundred of them, including Lord Strathmore, scuttled off to safety on the Isle of May. Bad weather stranded them there for several days. Highlanders were soon squabbling with Lowlanders, and all of the troops were pestering the fifteen fisher folk families who then lived on the May, for food and water. Eventually, the Royal Navy ships were blown out to sea by the gales, and Strathmore's troops finally managed to head back to their Perth headquarters, leaving the villagers of the Isle of May in peace. The Rebellion of 1715 failed, and James Stuart left Scotland only a few weeks later, sailing from Montrose, never to return.

The exploits of Bonny Prince Charlie during the 1745 Jacobite rising seem not to have affected the May in any way, nor does it appear to have become involved in the Napoleonic Wars. It has been said that the vertical slots in the walls of the Coal House near Kirkhaven landing may have been cut there for rifles, to enable the building to be used as a blockhouse guarding the Kirkhaven landing, had Napoleon ever attempted to invade the Isle of May. However, this coalhouse was built, not for the original beacon's fuel supply, but for the coal-fired steam-generated electricity for the Main Light, and this was not installed until 1885, long after Napoleon's time. If these slots do have any defensive purpose, they probably date from WWI.

World War 1

Because of its strategic position in the Firth of Forth, there was a military and/or naval presence on the May during the first World War from 1914 to 1918, but curiously enough, the secrecy that sometimes surrounds such establishments seems to have obscured almost all the records of who these men were, and precisely what their tasks may have been. All that I have been able to unearth about this period is that there was a small Signal Station on the brow of the island, close to the old beacon. This was manned by coastguard personnel, and used to relay to the mainland, messages concerning shipping passing the island. From time to time too, they were also able to give warning of German Zeppelin airships, which appeared to make regular use of the distinctive shape of the Isle of May as a visual fix, before heading farther west on their bombing missions. There was also a WWI gun battery with a field of fire that covered Kirkhaven landing place. This was located on the highest point in Chapel Field, a little to the south of the Chapel enclosure. For some period during WWI, Forth river pilots were based on the Isle of May, initially using the old beacon building as their somewhat spartan quarters, but later accommodated in huts erected on Thistle Field. Two of the Forth Estuary's fleet of RN motor torpedo boats (MTBs) were also based on the May from time to time between 1914 and 1918. The only visible reminder now of these vessels ever having been on the May consists of a wooden grave marker inscribed "WUFFY" of HMTB 28, drowned 25.X.14, presumably marking the burial place of a pet dog that once belonged to a sailor of the Royal Navy based on the May.

Within two months after the start of WWI, the Isle of May saw its first naval action. A light cruiser of the Royal Navy, HMS *Pathfinder*, was passing the Isle of May when it claimed the doubtful distinction of becoming the first warship ever to be sunk by a torpedo fired by a submarine, in this case a German U-boat. From time to time during WWI considerable U-boat activity took place around the May, culminating in an attempt by the Germans to seal off the Royal Navy fleet based at Rosyth by laying a half-moon shaped minefield across the entrance to the Firth, quite close to the Isle of May. British minesweepers thwarted this attempt.

Just off the shore of the island at the end of January 1918 one of the strangest and most tragic episodes in the history of the Royal Navy took place. This was wrapped in secrecy for a long time after it occurred and the Secretary of the Admiralty at the time, when questioned about it denied vehemently that it had ever happened. It does not even rate a mention in the official history of British naval operations in WWI, however most of the facts about what came to be known as the Battle of the Isle of May are now fairly well known.

The Battle of the Isle of May

On the night of 31 January 1918, a naval force including several battleships and cruisers, numerous destroyers and nine K-boats set sail under cover of darkness from Rosyth, near Dunfermline. In two

British Royal Navy K Class submarine, the type involved in the Battle of the Isle of May.

flotillas, they proceeded down the Forth, under the railway bridge, and east towards the North Sea. The K-boats mentioned were the Royal Navy's largest class of submarine; big boats, three times heavier than any other RN submarines of that time. Each carried 53 men, ten torpedo tubes, two 4" naval guns and one 3" anti-aircraft gun. The naval authorities suspected that one or more German U-boats were in the

Firth of Forth, and so ordered the British ships to sail without showing navigation lights, and to maintain radio silence.

As the first flotilla was approaching the Isle of May, cruising on the surface, the look-outs on K-11 and K-17 spotted a group of minesweepers ahead, and turned to port to avoid them. When the captain of K-14 eventually spotted through the darkness that K-17 had turned, and then saw two of the minesweepers ahead, he ordered K-14 to turn hard to starboard to avoid a collision. Unfortunately, the rudder of K-14 then jammed full right, and the K-boat continued to turn in a full circle. This took K-14 broadside into the path of its sister submarine K-22 which rammed into it at 19 knots. K-22's bows were badly damaged, and K-14's bows were sliced off. By sealing off watertight bulkheads, the crews managed to keep both submarines afloat. But they were now stopped in the water, without lights, and with the first flotilla of cruisers bearing down on them.

Three battle-cruisers swept majestically past, only rolling the crippled subs in their wake, but then a fourth, HMS *Inflexible* smashed straight into K-22, then rode over her, forcing her right under the surface. A few moments passed, then K-22 re-emerged from under the wake of *Inflexible*. Not unnaturally, both damaged vessels then switched on their navigation lights and broke radio silence, calling for help. HMS *Ithuriel* and several other ships turned back in the darkness to try to help them. Unfortunately this meant that these ships were now heading west, directly towards the second flotilla which was still steaming east.

HMS *Fearless*, leading the second flotilla, was unaware that the first flotilla had turned and, once east of the Isle of May at 7.54 pm its captain increased the flotilla's speed to 21 knots. Then both groups of ships met in the darkness, head-on just east of the May. At 8.32 pm, HMS *Fearless* struck the K-17 and sank her. The crew escaped the sinking sub, and stayed close together in the water, awaiting rescue by one of the nearby ships. But utter chaos ensued.

Behind *Fearless*, K-3 and K-4 stopped, but not before striking each other. Then K-6 had to swerve, to avoid being struck by HMS *Australia*, but in doing so, K-6 rammed into the K-4, almost slicing her in two. K-4 rolled inverted, and sank, taking her entire crew to the bottom with her. By now, the other capital ships and destroyers of the 5th Battle Squadron were bearing down on the scene, at 21 knots. Two of them narrowly missed K-3, and their wake swept every man off the deck of K-7, so they too had to be rescued. And finally, the escorting destroyers ploughed across the spot where K-17 had gone down, right through the pitiful cluster of fifty survivors from K-17, hopefully awaiting rescue from the sea. All but nine of these sailors were either chopped to pieces by the propellers or sucked down by the wake and drowned. And one of those nine died soon after being picked up by the deck crew of the K-7. Altogether the Battle of the Isle of May, in which not a single enemy ship took part, cost the Royal Navy two major submarines sunk, several other submarines and surface ships severely damaged, and the lives of at least 105 men.

One can understand why the Lords of the Admiralty did their best to hush the calamity up.

The wrecks of two WWI K-type submarines on the sea bottom became known by scuba divers as interesting underwater sites to visit, during the 1970s. Both submarines lie a little to the north-east of the Isle of May. It is possible for scuba divers to see inside the bent and broken conning tower of one of the subs, but the hull of the other sub is broken in two, and both are lying on a muddy bottom. (For more details see Chapters 8 and 9.)

Shortly after Armistice Day on 11 November 1918 the servicemen, lighthouse keepers and everyone else on the Isle of May witnessed a magnificent sight. Passing close to the shores of the island were many of the surrendered warships of the German Navy's High Seas Fleet, which were being escorted into the Firth of Forth by the mighty battleships and cruisers of the Royal Navy's Grand Fleet. It was some weeks after this that the captured German vessels were taken to Scapa Flow in the Orkney Islands for internment, but scuttled there by their German crews.

Following publication of the first edition of this book, the author received considerable correspondence about the "Battle of the Isle of May". As a result of this some corrections have been made to the details given in this Chapter of the terrible events that occurred off the Isle of May on the night of 31st January 1918.

Renewed interest in the "Battle" also led to the erection, on 31st January 2002, of a memorial plinth and bronze plaque commemorating those who lost their lives on that tragic occasion. This is located beside the car park opposite the Scottish Fisheries Museum in Anstruther, within sight of the Isle of May where these men lost their lives. The only other commemoration of the "Battle" that exists is a memorial in St Margaret Patten's Church, Cheapside, London to the men who died on board the submarine K4. This was erected by the widow of K4's Commanding Officer, Commander David DeBeauvoir Stokes, RN.

World War 2

Nothing quite so catastrophic as the Battle of the Isle of May took place on or near the island during WW2, but the May was the scene of a significant amount of mainly naval activity between 1939 and 1945. There still remain, in 2000, quite a few pieces of visible evidence to indicate something of what went on here, in these wartime days.

Already by 1938, with war clouds looming over Europe, the Royal Navy decided that the Isle of May would have to play an important strategic role in the defences of the Firth of Forth. Its position made it an ideal place to base measures to try to prevent enemy submarines and surface warships from penetrating from the North Sea past the island, then heading west, and threatening the important ports of Methil, Granton, Leith and above all, the Royal Navy's vast dockyard and other installations at Rosyth. The Admiralty ordered the laying on the sea bed of two lines of looped cable, one from the Isle of May to the Fife shore, the other from the island to the East Lothian shore. This series of indicator loops was initially not connected to anything on the island. Instead, the necessary control station for the system was held in store at Rosyth, but ready to be connected up for action whenever required. After the Munich crisis in 1938, the Admiralty requisitioned the entire Isle of May, and started restoring the WW1 signal station mentioned above, and building some accommodation huts.

Little happened for a year or so, but then, on 22 August 1939, just one week before the declaration of war, an order was given to bring the Firth of Forth's anti-submarine defences into immediate readiness. The portable loop control station was shipped from Rosyth to the Isle of May, connected up to the cables leading from the underwater indicator loops, and installed in a long wooden hut. This was erected in Fluke Street, within the natural fault that crosses the island from Kirkhaven to the Loch. The hut was built with three rooms. One contained the monitoring equipment for the loops and asdic; one was a wireless telegraphy office; and the third contained two diesel generators, to provide electric power for the whole system.

Spitfire's First Victory

The first action of WW2 to occur near the Isle of May did not involve it directly. On 16 October 1939, the first German air raid on the British mainland took place, with an attack on the Forth bridge and the Rosyth dockyards by Luftwaffe Junkers Ju 88 bombers. They flew over the May en route towards their targets, but could not be attacked, as the Isle of May never was equipped with any anti-aircraft guns, throughout WW2. (The only armament ever available on the island was a single Lewis gun,

A Luftwaffe Junkers Ju 8, of the type that became the RAF's first German victim over Britain during WW2. It crashed into the Firth of Forth near the Isle of May.

mounted beside the signal mast, plus a few rifles and revolvers.) The *Luftwaffe* aircraft were pounced upon by Spitfires as they were trying to sink HMS *Repulse* and HMS *Southampton* which were lying off Rosyth. One Junkers Ju 88, piloted by Helmut Pohle, was pursued, attacked and finally shot down into the sea between Crail and the Isle of May by a Spitfire of 602 Squadron, RAFVR, flown by Flt Lt George Pinkerton. This was the very first German aircraft to be shot down over Britain during WW2, so the RAF's first aerial victory of the war was achieved right beside the Isle of May. With the chivalry typical of the early days of WW2 aerial warfare, Pinkerton visited Pohle in hospital a few days later, bringing with him a present of a box of toffees. Helmut Pohle might have appreciated these sweets more, if only his front teeth hadn't been knocked out when his doomed Junkers had ditched into the Firth of Forth, close to the Isle of May.

As all the technical equipment was being fitted up and connected on the May, the island suddenly found itself becoming the rather isolated base for up to around 50 naval personnel. Some of these were Royal Naval Volunteer Reserve men, others Royal Navy pensioners, recalled for duty. These were in addition to the lighthouse men and their families, and in December 1941 they were joined by six members of the Royal Observer Corps, a detachment from Dunfermline ROC, to report all aircraft movements sighted from the island. The Isle of May hadn't seen so many people living on it since the village was abandoned, two centuries earlier.

Earlier in 1941 there had been another flurry of activity connected with aviation, just off the Isle of May, after a prototype de Havilland Mosquito crashed into the Firth. The Air Ministry did not wish any fragments of the aircraft's unusual balsawood construction to fall into enemy hands, and arranged for trawlers and fishing boats to try to salvage every scrap of wreckage that came to the surface. The remnants of the Mosquito's engines and undercarriage are believed to be still lying a little offshore, east of the May.

Anti-submarine Defences

The line of defence for the Firth of Forth that was based on the Isle of May was known to most people along the Fife and Lothian coasts as "the boom". As a schoolboy, I remember finding this a puzzling title, and wondering who it was that opened and closed "the boom" to allow the frequent movement of convoys and naval ships into and out of the Firth. In fact the indicator loop system was actually an electro-magnetic system lying on the sea bed. It detected the movement of all shipping sailing across it. German U-boats and small surface vessels were expected to be the principal threat to the ports and shipping in the Forth, and the "basalt battleship" into which the May was transformed in WW2 had one main duty. This was the detection, identification and recording of all vessels entering or leaving the Firth of Forth. It was also to act as a communications link between these vessels and the Royal Navy at Rosyth. For naval administrative purposes, the island became a satellite of the RN depot ship HMS *Cochrane II* at Rosyth.

Early in 1940, a second line of loops was laid on the sea bed, about one mile away from the first. Via Cable Cleft and Horse Hole on the island, the outer loop line stretched to a point just offshore, near Crail in Fife. In the other direction, it led from Pilgrims Haven on the Isle of May, via the east of the Bass Rock, to a terminal in Canty Bay, just east of North Berwick in East Lothian. The inner line ran from Horse Hole to a point close to the Fife coast near Cellardyke, and from Pilgrims Haven via the west of the Bass Rock, again to Canty Bay. The ends of the loop cables did not actually come ashore in Fife or Lothian; their only connection was with the Isle of May.

This double system made it possible for the men on the May to monitor not only when a vessel crossed the line, but also to estimate its speed and course. The passage of any iron or steel hulled ship over the loops caused a change in the magnetic

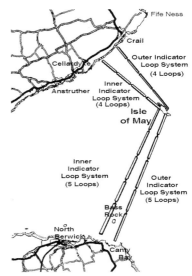

Approximate location of the four lines of electro-magnetic loop detectors connected to the Isle of May that were used by the Royal Navy during WW2 to plot the movements of all ships and submarines entering and leaving the Firth of Forth.

field, and this generated a small electric current in the loop directly beneath the vessel. In the control room on the Isle of May, this was amplified, and then recorded by a zig-zag movement of a pen recorder, which otherwise traced a steady straight line onto a slowly-moving roll of graph paper. Each loop had a number, and each zig-zag was plotted above that section of the line. When the vessel crossed the second line, the position of the next zig-zag and the time between them indicated its course and speed. Every time a crossing was detected, the operators notified the signal station staff, who had a wooden look-out tower on top of the signal station flat roof, and normally identified the vessel visually.

Most wartime shipping was notified in advance and most merchant ships moved in convoys, whose escort identified the convoy to the May. When vessels couldn't be identified, due to Haar or darkness perhaps, two other lines of defence were called into action, in case the vessel was an enemy intruder on or below the surface. The commander of the May could call on a fleet of armed anti-submarine trawlers based at Granton, and five drifters, originally from Buckie but then based at Anstruther. Two or three of these were on 24-hour constant patrol, just west of and inside the loop system and whenever an unidentified crossing occurred they were alerted by radio to investigate. Simultaneously, the Isle of May's Harbour Defence Asdic (HDA) came into service. HDA was an early form of sonar, and detected submarines by an echo-sounding system. Connected to the control room on the Isle of the May were six Asdic domes anchored to the sea bed, just west of the loop lines. These produced "pings" which were echoed back off any submarines in the vicinity. In the control room, the bearings of each echo could be plotted and a range recorder plotted the target's range.

Special care had always to be exercised when convoys were crossing the lines, as this could provide an opportunity for a U-boat to sneak past, undetected, below them. There were many false alarms, mainly due to fishing boats putting out for some illegal fishing at night, but occasionally due to foreign ships failing to observe standard procedures for entering the Firth of Forth. Some of these ships had to be forced to stop by shells fired across their bows from the two 6-inch Mark VII guns of the battery mounted at Kincraig, near Elie. On at least one occasion a shell fired from Kincraig for this purpose ricocheted off the water, skimmed right across the Forth and exploded near North Berwick, to the considerable consternation of people living in the vicinity.

Radar Arrives

In spring 1942, a portable wooden cabin (called a Gibson Box) with a radar dish on top, was installed on the May, not far from the signal station. It contained a Type 31 surface watching radar. This greatly helped recording shipping in bad visibility and darkness. It was later augmented by a newer Type 41 radar, housed in a small brick building just west of the Type 31 unit. Another brick hut was erected beside Holyman's Road, slightly east of the radars. This building housed the engine and generator providing the radars with power. These radars were not designed for the detection of aircraft, but experiments were carried out on the May during 1943, to assess their effectiveness against aircraft. Supermarine Walrus amphibians flying from Donibristle aerodrome (a Royal Naval Air Station near Rosyth) and from Dunino RNAS near Kingsbarns, were used as target aircraft in these secret trials.

Most of the construction materials for the wartime buildings and installations came by sea from Rosyth, using a Landing Craft. To transport materials ashore, a tractor and trailer were stationed on the Isle of May. Supplies of food and fresh water were brought from Anstruther on two fishing boats of the "Fifies" type, the *Refuge* and the *Royal Burghs*, which were under contract to the Admiralty. These boats provided as near as possible a daily service, weather permitting, and also conveyed men to and from the Isle of May. The fresh water could only be brought ashore at Kirkhaven when the seas were relatively calm, as it had to be pumped from there into two lime-washed storage tanks. The May was regarded as an unusual, but none too arduous a posting. Discipline was fairly slack, uniform seldom worn (other then for Church Parades), and rations were good. Navy food was often augmented by locally trapped rabbits, fish caught from the rowing boat they had at their disposal, herring gull eggs, and lobsters caught in pots purchased from local fishermen. The navy even reared a pig on the island, and had a supply of fresh goat milk from the lighthouse keepers' herd.

Although the lighthouse did not operate constantly in wartime, but only at the specific request of ships (and even then usually at low power) it still had to be fully manned. For the duration of the war, the lighthouse keepers and their families were evicted from their usual houses in Fluke Street, and moved instead into the main lighthouse building. The Observer Corps men were accommodated in the rooms beside the Low Light (now used by bird watchers). The Naval officers occupied the lighthouse families' normal residences in Fluke Street, where their wardroom was also established. Naval ratings, Petty Officers and CPOs were accommodated in three concrete-floored wooden huts in Thistle Field, overlooking Kirkhaven. These contained sleeping quarters, a galley and toilet facilities. In 1942 an extra Nissen Hut was erected and this served as a canteen and recreation area.

About 1942, someone realised that this whole Firth of Forth defence system based on the May could be shut down by a single bomb exploding anywhere near the wooden control hut, and therefore, substantial bomb-proof brick walls and a reinforced concrete roof were built, enclosing the hut on three sides. The fourth side of the hut was so close to the rock cliff-face that it required no further protection. Like the remnants of the radar buildings, this protective wall is one of the few wartime constructions on the Isle of May still easy for visitors to recognise. Throughout the war, however, the virtually unarmed Isle of May remained vulnerable to attack by an armed landing party from a U-boat or from another type of enemy ship. Fortunately for its garrison, such an attack was never attempted.

Sinkings by U-boats

In fact, the existence of the complex loop system seems to have been known to the German Navy, and there is no confirmed record of any enemy ship having tried to penetrate into the Firth, until the very last days of the War. A crossing was detected in the control room, quite close to the south end of the Isle of May. No surface vessel was visible, so the anti-submarine trawlers were alerted and the Asdics switched on. A second zig-zag on the pen recorders soon indicated that the intruder was passing the inner line of loops, and it was suspected that a U-boat must be trying to float silently past on the incoming tide. Destroyers arrived at the May and began dropping depth charges under instructions from the control room on the May, but no oil and no sign of wreckage was seen. The search continued all night, but no trace of the submarine was seen until early next morning, when the loop system detected it crossing first the inner and then the outer line again.

Another search by trawlers and destroyers was again fruitless, but the vessel detected was almost certainly the same submarine that caused one of the last dramas of the European part of WW2, just 30 minutes before VE day, at 2330 on 7 May 1945. Two merchant ships leaving the Firth of Forth were less than one mile off the south-east corner of the May when suddenly both were struck by torpedoes and sank, within a few minutes of each other. Of the crews, fifty-five survived, but two men from the British *SS Avondale Park* and seven from the Norwegian *SS Snayland* were lost. Their attacker was a Type XXIII U-boat U-2336 whose commander, Kapitänleutnant Klusmeier, later claimed that he had known nothing about the war ending. They had received no radio messages at all since the time the U-2336 had departed from its U-boat base in Kiel one week earlier.

Navy life on the May

Lieutenant Commander Rolph Griffiths, who was officer in command of the May from summer 1944 (when he took over from Lt Cdr Robert Williams) until the RN finally lost interest in the May in February 1946, enjoyed his period as OIC *"HMS Isle of May"*. He developed a keen interest in the bird life and was a sort of honorary warden, putting the main breeding areas out of bounds to all his men during the sensitive nesting seasons. One of the few problems he encountered was when his radar Petty Officer was injured and had to be sent ashore to hospital. The urgent signal to Rosyth for a relief was answered when a gorgeous-looking blonde WREN Petty Officer stepped ashore at Kirkhaven off the supply Fifie. Not having any segregated other ranks quarters, the OIC decided, (probably to the considerable chagrin of many of the seamen) to billet the girl in the lighthouse keepers' quarters, with the keeper's wife delegated to act as chaperone.

Lt Cdr Griffith's little daughter Joan also made a small piece of history when she was christened within the ruins of St Adrian's Priory in August 1945. That was the first such ceremony to take place there for over a century. The Rev James Paterson, minister of Anstruther Wester Church (within whose parish the island lies) and Naval Chaplain Malcolm MacPherson from Rosyth officiated. The "ship's company" were present and the baby's health was toasted in Navy rum in the wardroom in Fluke Street.

The first edition of this book was well received and generated considerable correspondence, much of which has been incorporated into this edition. Among the interesting letters received by the author was one from a Mrs Mary Brown who in WW2 was Petty Officer Mary Cochran, the "gorgeous looking blonde WREN" referred to above. The photograph fowarded to the autor by her daughter confirms just why the OIC of the Isle of May had deemed it necessary to have her chaperoned by the lighthouse keeper's wife

Chapter 8
Religious and Other Remains

From the time that the English navy started to ransack the buildings on the Isle of May until very recently, the remains of the priory and its surroundings were regarded as little more than objects of vague curiosity. At times they were used as convenient sources of building materials for other structures, including parts of the first lighthouse (although most of this consists of local rubble), some of the cottages in the village, smugglers' hiding places and the foundations of the WWl signal station. But during the 1990s, this site became a focal point of interest for archaeologists eager to examine the remains and use them to add to our knowledge of the history of the Isle of May and the people who have been connected with it over the centuries.

Big Dig in the Nineties

For five years between 1992 and 1997, teams of archaeologists led by Fife Council (initially Fife Regional Council) in partnership with Scottish Natural Heritage, spent several months each summer carefully excavating and mapping the ancient edifices and the ground in their vicinity. Gradually they managed to piece together much of

Reconstruction drawing showing the probable appearance of the Manor House into which the west wing of the old monastery of the Isle of May was converted during the 16th century. (Illustration reproduced by permission of the Archaeological Unit of Fife Council Planning Service).

what we today know about the many different phases these buildings went through. The excavations also have shown us something about how early farming communities of what now is Fife may already have been making use of the resources of the Isle of May, many centuries before the missionaries arrived. Pieces of pottery, flint arrow-heads and a polished stone axe-head have all been found on the island. The earliest piece that has so far been dated, is a broken shard of pottery that was made during the Bronze Age, probably around 2000 BC. Even earlier than that, our ancestors almost certainly used their coracles to fish the waters around the May. They would also help provide for their families by collecting seabird eggs there, and by killing birds and seals for food and skins.

One of the aims of the archeology project on the May was, of course, to find evidence from the time of the early Christian use of the island, especially from the time of St Adrian himself. North of the remains of the old monastic church, a graveyard was excavated. Among the oldest burials found were some in shallow graves known as "long cists", panelled with stone slabs and neatly aligned in rows. Radiocarbon dating showed that some of these originated in the 5th century AD, and possibly even earlier. In other words, burials were taking place on the May at least 200 years before the first Christians arrived. Together with these burials, the archeologists found many white quartz pebble stones. It is known from elsewhere that quartz pebbles are a traditional grave offering found with much older prehistoric burials, and this leads one to wonder whether the later Christian burials on the May were simply maintaining a millennia-old tradition.

Between these ancient graves and the site of the late church, the excavations uncovered an extraordinary large burial cairn, at least 25 metres (80 feet) long and about 20 metres (65 feet) wide. Its sides had revetment wall reinforcements and many of the hundreds of burials it contains were covered with piles of beach stones and new graves later placed on top. It is certainly the largest platform cairn from this period to have been discovered anywhere in Scotland, and may well have served as the original resting place of St Adrian and his fellow monks after their murder by the Danish Vikings.

Part of this cairn has been used to form the foundation for what seems to have been a church, possibly built in the 11th century to house the relics of the martyred St Adrian. This would make it one of the earliest known churches in the country. Its dry-stone foundations are similar to those of 7th to 10th century churches in Ireland. When, as described in Chapter 3, the Benedictine monks arrived on the Isle of May from Reading at the behest of King David I, they appear to have used this pre-existing church while getting on with constructing their own Priory buildings. and only later enlarged the old church to form their own place of worship. Excavations have proved that the monastery on the May was built in the style current at that time, comprising four main buildings around a central open cloister. Their church itself was to the north, beside the burial ground, to the east they had a meeting room and cellar, and on an upper-floor, the monks' dormitory. To the south was the refectory or dining room and next to it, the west range with private accommodation for the prior. At the rear of the dormitory an unusual communal closet was discovered, with holes provided for no fewer than ten monastic bottoms. Since the monks seldom numbered more than ten, and since they would be most unlikely all to want to use the toilet at the same time, the archaeologists concluded that this must have been a facility provided for pilgrims visiting the May from around the 12th century.

Before the archeologists started their excavation work on the May, only some vestiges of the west range of the monastery were visible above ground. Now visitors can see the lines of the walls of all four main buildings. Traces of where the drains ran have been identified, and cylindrical stones that once were parts of the pillars supporting the roofs. Bits of greenish glass from the windows, roofing stone slates that were brought from an Angus quarry, sandstone lintels from Craighead near Crail, candle-stick bases, green-glazed ceramic floor-tiles and artistically carved masonry, all help us now to understand the conditions in which these monks lived and worked in the 12th and 13th centuries. Bones and other remnants in their kitchen middens betray something about what victuals they ate. Cod, saith, seabirds and rabbits, together with the staple diet of cereals brought across from the farmland they owned in mainland Fife.

Archaeological examination of these buildings has revealed that, after the monks departed the May and took up residence in Pittenweem, the west building of the old monastery was refurbished and transformed into a small manor house, probably sometime in the 16th century. This house appears to have had an impressive round tower added to the medieval walls, on its south-west corner.

Signs have now been put in place to help visitors understand what they are seeing, in these remnants of ancient walls and graves.

Understanding what's left of the Beacon

Central on the island, the cut-down stump of the original lighthouse (as described in Chapter 6) still stands, amid its surrounding area of henbane and grass struggling to survive on the piles of ash that are all that remains of all the 60,000 tons of coal that was burnt in its brazier over its 180 years in service. The interior of this beacon is not normally accessible to visitors, but after being truncated when the new light was completed, it was used for a time as a guardroom by Forth pilots and fishermen. This use came to an end around the start of WWI and

Above the dilapidated fireplace inside the old Beacon, the initials A. C. of its builder Alexander Cunnynghame can still be distinguished on the chimney-piece frieze.

since then the only practical use of the Beacon has been as a store for the lighthouse keepers. Its entrance and only window face south, the door opening into a small lobby with a sealed-off stairway. There is a panel above the door, with the date 1636, two bits of a heraldic water-spout and the sun in glory. This possibly may originally have been on the upper part of the tower. Inside the building there is a fireplace on the north wall, and a corniced chimney-piece frieze with the initials "A. C." and a coat of arms, presumably that of Alexander Cunnynghame.

Vanished Village of the May

Although contemporary descriptions of the Isle of May from around the late 19th century mention that it was then still possible to see traces of the houses of the village that once existed in the island, no vestige of them seems to be visible now. The writer has tried in vain by means of aerial photography to distinguish where the village may have been and archaeologists have attempted the same task on the ground, with equal lack of success. Now all that seems to remain as a reminder of the old village is the solitary broken gravestone mentioned in Chapter 3.

The Main Lighthouse

Just a few metres west of the Beacon is the unmistakable Tower, or main lighthouse, with its accommodation for three families (again described in Chapter 6). Close to it can be seen the walled gardens that were once used by the resident lighthouse families to grow vegetables and flowers. Most of the soil in these plots has been brought in from elsewhere, as there are few places in the May with any real depth of fertile cover over the rock. Between the Tower and the keepers' gardens you can see what is left of a large ornamental sundial. Also connected with the operation of this Tower are most of the buildings still standing in Fluke Street; the engine room, lighthouse men's houses, the compressor buildings, the dam, and its freshwater loch. Metal pipelines run from the compressor buildings, over ground for the most part, to both the South Horn (built in 1886 and replaced by a new horn in a better position in 1918) and the North Horn (built in 1938-39).

North and South Horns

The booming sound of the Isle of May fog horns was produced by compressed air. The compressors were in the old Boiler House in Fluke Street, and were cooled by water drawn from the loch. The compressed air was stored in the huge red-painted metal reservoir tanks that still stand alongside the compressor house and, whenever air was needed to operate the horns in foggy weather conditions, it was fed from these tanks via steel pipelines to both the north and south ends of the island.

Close to the South Horn stands an unusual tall concrete edifice, looking for all the world like a telephone kiosk built for the use of giants. (To complete the illusion, there seems even to be a shelf for a huge phone to sit on.) This once contained the control mechanism for the original horn, a system that resembled a grandfather clock, in which weights slowly turned ratchet wheels and opened the valve allowing compressed air to sound the horn at the prescribed intervals. When the weights neared the ground, another valve was opened, compressed air blew against a sort of turbine which rewound the clock, and the whole sequence started again. The original South Horn which used this mechanism was built in 1886, but proved to be too low down for the sound of the horn to carry. The 1918 replacement Horn (which visitors can still see today) was located in a higher position. The control mechanisms of the rebuilt South Horn and of the North Horn are concealed within the bases of the horns themselves.

This concrete construction close to the South Horn may look like a giant's telephone box, but it used to house the pneumatic mechanism that controlled the timing of the horn.

In foggy weather, the South Horn used to blare out four blasts of two-and-a-half seconds each in quick succession, every 2 minutes and 15 seconds. Midway between these sets of lugubrious warning notes the North Horn blew its steady seven-second mournful sound, also at intervals of 2 minutes and 15 seconds. For many decades, the sound of the Isle of May's two foghorns was very much part of life in the East Neuk villages, where it could be clearly heard every time the East Haar descended on the Firth.

Marks left by the Royal Navy

In addition to the bomb protection walls and reinforced concrete roof of the WW2 control cabin in Fluke Street and the remnants of the radar buildings (described in Chapter 7), there are still quite a few other visible reminders of the part the Isle of May played in WW2. Not far from the Tower, you can see several large concrete anchor blocks with metal lugs in them, protruding from the ground. These were the stays helping to prevent the Navy's wartime signal mast and radio masts from being blown down in the gales that sweep across the island. Some rusty turnbuckles formerly used to tension these rigging wires were still in evidence there in 2000.

The concrete foundations of the Royal Navy's accommodation huts and their Nissen Hut canteen are all still visible in the picnic area in front of the visitor centre and information hut, close to Kirkhaven. There are also some patches of ground to the west of Holyman's Road that are polluted by brown iron oxide, where virtually nothing grows. These areas of rust still contain some short sections of badly-corroded steel cables, and this is almost certainly where the WW2 anti-submarine loop system was cut up after the war, and left to rust away in the salty air. Now, after over 60 years, this process of decay is almost complete.

The former boiler house (now with hot-water solar panels on its roof) and the keepers' house in Fluke Street. Behind the keepers' houses the bomb-proof shelter built around the Royal Navy's WW2 loop system control cabin can still be seen.

The two WW2 radar huts can be seen standing just a few metres apart, downhill from but not far to the east of the Beacon. In the concrete roof of one, the hole cut through for the drive and wiring to the radar scanner mounted on top of the hut can still be seen. The foundations of the radar generator building, including the mounting block for the engine, is just west of the upper of the two radar huts.

At Altarstanes landing there are several remnants of a steel landing platform used by the Royal Navy when larger ships than the regular fishing boats were used to bring personnel or supplies to the island. Most of the steelwork has gone, but rusty marks on pieces of concrete and metal stubs anchored to the rock can still be seen.

The concrete disc with the painted "H" on it, to the west of the main Tower light and the old Beacon, is a helicopter landing pad, and is of much more recent origin.

Around the Isle of May there are many other remains, the remains of shipping that has come to grief on or near the island's coast. A few pieces of wreckage from some of these (e.g. the *Mars* and the *Island*) are visible to keen-eyed visitors walking the paths on the Isle of May, but many, many more lie concealed from all eyes (except those of divers) beneath the waves of the Firth of Forth.

Wrecks around the Isle of May

One of the easiest of these for scuba divers to locate and visit is the wreck of the *Anlaby*, a British coal-carrying cargo ship which ran aground in fog, in August 1893. It lies just off Altarstanes, in about 18 metres of water. The ship is now badly broken up, but with her propeller and rudder still visible, extending from her rusty iron ribs. Less than half a mile south-west of the May the remains of a steel-hulled fishing trawler lie 30 metres deep on a silty bottom. She was the *Primrose*, which sank in 1904. Although much of the superstructure has disintegrated, the hull is still in reasonable condition.

Along the east coast of the island there are many wrecks which divers can explore

The Danish steamship Island photographed shortly after it ran aground on the Isle of May in 1937. Parts of its wreckage are still visible.

in waters which are generally better sheltered and with fewer strong currents to contend with. The steamship *Scotland* came to grief in 1916 on the rocks known as the Pillow, not far from Kirkhaven harbour, and divers believe that wreckage scattered near there is from that ship. Much of that wreck is still undiscovered. Beyond Foreigner's Point, close to where the remains of the Danish *Island* are visible on the rocks, divers can see more of her remains on the sea bed at depths of between 15 and 20 metres. Foreigner's Point owes its name to another shipwreck, that of the *Newcastle Packet*, on her way from Kristiansand to Grangemouth in 1889, carrying timber. The foreigner involved here was her Norwegian skipper, who terrified a lighthouse man's family by knocking on their bedroom window at 2 o'clock in the morning, shouting in a language incomprehensible to them.

Farther north, beyond East Tarbet, pieces of the *SS Jasper* can be seen. She ran aground on the May in 1894, and broke up in shallow water. Close to these remains lies the schooner *Linnet*, which sank in 1877. Then, the north end of Rona, around Mars Rocks, Norman Rock and Shag Rock is a true graveyard of shipping. Wrecks here include the Latvian steamer *Mars*, which ran aground on 19 May 1936 on her way to Methil to load coal; the three-masted schooner *Matagarda*, which struck the east side of North Ness on 3 April 1872; a Granton-based fishing trawler called *Thomas L Devlin*, which hit the Ness on 20 December 1959 on her way home for

Christmas with a good catch in her holds; and the steamship *George Aunger*, which ran aground in fog on 25 April 1930.

Slightly farther out from the Isle of May, divers have examined the *SS Mallard*, about a mile offshore, which sank while carrying coal from Dysart to Peterhead, and the trawler *Northumbria*, which struck a mine in 1917 and sank 33 metres to the bottom. Not much of her is identifiable, other than her steam boilers. Also, the two ships mentioned in Chapter 7 as being the last to be torpedoed before VE day in 1945, both lie about a mile and a half offshore, in fairly deep water. Divers say the wreck of the *Avondale Park* is a spectacular one to visit, but requires experience, due to the 55 metre depth involved. At similar depths are the remains of two WWI German U-boats sunk close to the May, the U-36 and the U-12.

Finally, as mentioned in Chapter 7, divers frequently visit the wrecks of two of the British K-class submarines that sank during the Battle of the Isle of May in January 1918. Both wrecks are lying about 55 metres down, on a muddy bottom, north-east of the island. The K-4 is lying in two pieces, whith her hull broken asunder, but the K-17 is more intact, although her conning tower is bent over and has split open. This allows divers to see something of what is inside the old submarine, including the control panel, and piles of crockery, cups and dinner plates, still stacked on top of each other.

Chapter 9
Sailing, Diving, Flying, Climbing etc

A general guide book like this is not the place to look for technical information about navigation, harbour entry, safety precautions or other professional matters. These subjects are fully dealt with in specialist publications for yachtsmen, scuba divers, private pilots, and participants in other outdoor sports and activities. The intention of this Chapter is simply to give a brief introduction to what the Isle of May has and has not, to offer to visitors whose interests may lie along these lines.

There are two recognised landing places in the Isle of May for private boats, yachts and inflatables. These are at Kirkhaven, the east landing, and at Altarstanes, the west landing. The choice of which to use can depends mainly on the type of boat involved, and on the sea conditions prevailing at the time. All of the island's attractions are within easy walking distance of either. Kirkhaven is undoubtedly the more sheltered

of the two alternatives, but when approaching it special care must be taken to use the two white beacons near the South Horn to line your craft up with the correct inlet and then to keep straight within the harbour by using the next pair of white markers as you sail towards the pier. There are several "skellies" or reefs and rocks lying under water, in wait for the unwary skipper.

Diving the May

For persons coming to the May to dive around its coasts, there are, of course, many other little bays and inlets where inflatables can be moored, closer to the underwater places of interest. However, especially during the breeding season, divers are asked to keep a respectable distance from the cliffs, to ensure that the seabirds nesting there are not disturbed. Another important precaution for the island's bird life, is to approach at a reasonably slow speed in your RHIBs and inflatables, and to watch out for and avoid the flocks of birds (principally puffins, eiders, guillemots and razorbills) which are frequently to be found resting in the sea around the May. In addition to the danger of colliding with and injuring the birds, an inconsiderately handled boat will disturb them and interrupt what is an important part of their life cycle, so threatening their well-being.

It is also important to avoid disturbing the seal population, especially during the pupping season, between October and December. Special permission is required to visit the May at this time (see Chapter 1) and if you fancy diving with the seals, you would probably be better to wait till the following summer. The young pups still around the island then can prove to be quite inquisitive creatures, sometimes coming close enough under water to let you tickle them under their chins.

The Isle of May is widely recognised as one of the best dive sites on the east coast of Scotland and is deservedly popular with scuba divers. RHIBs and inflatables can generally be launched during the six hour period around High Tide at Anstruther Harbour, using the lifeboat slip and paying the harbour master a launch fee. If a lifeboat call-out or exercise renders this slipway inaccessible, an alternative harbour for departure is at Cellardyke, just over one kilometre to the east. It is wise to advise the coastguard station at Fife Ness (telephone 01333 450666, or on Channels 16 & 67) of what your plans are and when you expect to return. They will also be happy to give you up-to-date weather and tide information if you require it.

There are strong tide races around both the North Ness and South Ness of the May. Slack water is about two hours after high water at Anstruther. Some careful planning is therefore required, to make the most of the limited launch period at Anstruther Harbour combined with the best times for diving off the May.

The visibility underwater can be good, especially in the months of May and June when you can expect to see 10 to 15 metres. It can be very good also after a longish period of calm weather during the winter. Plankton can, unfortunately, limit visibility at other times. There is still, however, a great deal to see and do diving around the Isle of May. Along the foot of the cliffs between Altarstanes and Pilgrims Haven there is some wonderful diving available. Between 10 and 20 metres, the bouldery slopes at the foot of Green Face are the home for conger eels, wolf fish and octopus, as well as lots of crabs and lobsters. Don't be surprised to meet bird life down here too. Guillemots often flash past you underwater, chasing shoals of small fish at incredible speed. Mill Door is a marvellous cave, about six metres underwater, with a window at one end, leading to the open sea. In calm conditions with little surge, it is quite safe to dive right through it. You will probably have some seals for company, as well as shoals of pollack and saithe. There are other caves too, some where seals often sleep at the top end, so approach these circumspectly.

The stacks called Angel and Pilgrim are near Pilgrims Haven and here you will see sponges, nudibranchs and sea anemones growing in profusion. Many boulders are covered in deadmen's fingers, and towards the south east end of the island there are

Scuba divers' inflatables off the Isle of May.

gullies leading to forests of kelp, then a drop down to 30 metres or so. Here you will find lobsters, rocks that are coloured pink with coral, and lots of large starfish. Another speciality of the west side bottom is a selection of large multi-coloured anemones.

Diving along the east side of the island is more sheltered from the prevailing wind and from tidal flows and surges. On the other hand, the sea life is less spectacular, although still interesting. In shallow water there are many chitons, and along the coast near the Low Light and Tarbet Hole a steep, stepped rock face leads down to a sandy bottom at 27 metres, with more dead man's fingers and, on the sand, a dense carpet of brittle stars. This area of brittle stars covers the entire east side of the May, below 25 metres.

Then, of course, there are all the pieces of wrecked ships to explore, and the occasional almost complete ship that although wrecked, unlike the chunks of debris, still looks like a ship where it lies on the bottom. For more details of these see Chapter 8.

Rock Climbing

In a word, don't.

Any keen rock climber who has been to the Isle of May must have itched to have a go at some of the spectacular sea cliffs on the island. Climbing here was once a popular pastime for visitors, many years ago. Some of the WW2 naval personnel stationed on the island also used to enjoy the challenge of ascending certain of the local cliffs, occasionally collecting herring gulls' eggs while doing so. [One of the Petty Officers regularly packed herring gulls' eggs in cases and sent them off to a hospital in London, to augment the meagre wartime egg ration for the patients.] Nowadays, however, in the interests of the seabirds breeding on all of the island's cliffs and sea stacks, no rock climbing whatsoever is permitted anywhere on the Isle of May.

Moreover, the greenstone of which the May is composed is not a particularly good climbing rock. In many places it is very friable, and can be quite treacherous. And any would-be climbers today can console themselves with the fact that these rocks are often extremely slippery with bird droppings. Old climbers say that this layer of guano always did make the May's cliffs both unsafe and unattractive for climbing, throughout most of the summer.

In the past, the 25 metre (80 feet) Angel sea stack used to be a magnet for climbers. To the eyes of an uninitiated visitor it looks impossibly dangerous and pretty well unscalable, but it has been conquered on numerous occasions. It has distinct overhangs, as the circumference at the base is appreciably smaller than the circumference of the pillar half way up it. Despite that, it was in fact not too difficult a climb, as far as the gap between the two summits, but tricky for the final few feet to either of the tops. Near the Angel too, the walls of Pilgrims Haven at one time also used to provide several short but challenging climbs on sound, if nearly vertical, rock. Other traverses and climbs of buttresses and cliffs have been made just south of Altarstanes, but as elsewhere, all of these potential scrambles are now of no more than academic interest to would-be climbers.

The Bishop sea stack, midway along the west coast of the May also looks as if it once presented some interesting technical challenges. In some ways it could be compared to a scaled-down Old Man of Hoy, in the Orkney Islands, and the view from the top of the Bishop must certainly have been magnificent.

The May from the Air

As mentioned in Chapter 1, there is no landing place for aircraft on the Isle of May, other than a pad for helicopters, use of which is generally reserved for flights made in connection with Lighthouse or Scottish Natural Heritage business. There is however, no special restriction placed on overflying the island in light aircraft, but the Isle of May lies just outside the western boundary of danger area D607/55, so care must be taken not to infringe this when it is active. The May makes an excellent subject for aerial photography, showing many different aspects and appearances as the light and your angle to it changes. It is also a place that always is of interest to passengers who love to see the dots of white on the far island transform themselves into lighthouses and horns, to identify the ruins of the priory, see the network of paths across the island and watch the swell breaking against the cliffs. The principle ground-level attractions of the island, its bird life and seals, cannot however, be enjoyed to any advantage from the air. Maintaining the legal minimum of 500 feet above the main lighthouse (which itself is 240 feet above the sea) means that most of the puffins and auks and gulls can be seen only as vague clouds of white dots against the sea - or black dots in the case of shags and some of the other birds. A good reason to return to see the island and its bird inhabitants in a less cursory fashion next time. Pilots should also remember that many seabirds often fly at heights well above 1,000 feet, and that a birdstrike can never be ruled out while you are flying in the vicinity of a dense bird population like that of the May.

There are five nautical miles of cold salt water between the Isle of May and the nearest mainland landing place, and precious little chance of bringing off a satisfactory forced landing on the May itself, should a mechanical problem strike. It is good practice to make sure that everyone on board is actually wearing a life jacket for the entire flight from coasting out from Fife (or East Lothian) until back over land again. Leuchars radar covers the area of the Isle of May well, and it is advisable to keep RAF Leuchars informed (on 126.50 MHz) of your movements. An average light aircraft could, in the event of engine failure over the Isle of May, glide safely back to the coast at Crail provided it was flying at 2,500 feet or above. It would therefore perhaps be more prudent, and kinder to the bird life below, to maintain at least that height throughout the trip, rather then coming down to around the legal minimum 500 feet when close to the island. Instead of low flying, better just use telephoto lenses for your photography.

Chapter 10
Links with America

There is only one Isle of May, anywhere in the world, so far as I have been able to confirm. Many other Scottish place-names have been duplicated in America, Australia, New Zealand and many of the other countries to which Scots have emigrated. But there still seems to be only one Isle of May.

And yet, I did once come across the name, thousands of miles away from the Firth of Forth. In the little town of Sausalito, across the famous Golden Gate bridge from San Francisco in northern California, there is a hotel known as the Casa Madrona that overlooks the waters of San Francisco Bay. And in the Casa Madrona is a restaurant which, rather mysteriously, is dedicated to "Mikayla, the Goddess of the Isle of May". On one of the restaurant walls is a 12-foot mural, painted by artist Laurel Burch, which depicts the story of Mikayla. According to the Casa Madrona, this is the legend of the Goddess, Mikayla.

> Long, long ago on the Isle of May, off the coast of the great Lost Continent, where the water meets the sky, dwelled a clan of soil tillers and gatherers, happy folk all. At the foot of their sacred Mount Lushlee, rising high into a crown of clouds, the villagers gathered during the waxing of the moon to celebrate their good fortune. They brought gifts of forage to the regal mountain, then danced throughout the night in pristine bliss.

> One dreadful day as they tilled and gathered, while father sun hung high in the sky, a resounding rumble shook the villagers to the ground. They looked up as the top of their cone-shaped mountain exploded, spewing forth fire and ash. Frightened, they jumped to their feet and fled the flaming stream of molten matter that flowed towards the sea in the direction of the setting sun. Once on the far side of the island, dejected and weary, they crowded together with voices dulled and grieved, whispered among themselves of their misfortune. Gone were their meadows and grasslands. How would they survive? They clasped their hands and made circles of five to pray to Mother Earth, keeper of the four elements.

> Many moons and suns rose and set before the islanders finally ceased their vigil. When they gazed out over the sea, a resplendent sight greeted them in the foggy mist. A tall goddess with eyes the colour of the sky arose from the foam. Shimmering sea shells dotted her golden braided hair and she wore a diaphanous gown entwined with seaweed. She lifted her hands in salutation, and in her hands she held two beautiful fish of rainbow hue. The villagers

stared in awe. The goddess waded from the depths of the sea and placed the fish on shore.

"These will sustain you," she said in a voice as soft as the gentle wind that lifted her hair and rippled the hem of her gown. "These are my gifts to you. Henceforth you will be known as the sons and daughters of Mikayla, they who scour the sea for their existence"

After that proclamation, the Goddess turned and made her way back to the deep waters. With a loving smile, she waved farewell and returned to the depths. The grateful islanders consumed Mikayla's gift, then proceeded to carve rough dug-outs to gather their own supply.

Not long after, they constructed a temple of stone, and on the highest pulpit erected a statue in Mikayla's honour: Sea Goddess of Nourishment.

It is a trite little tale, with several suggestions of other mythical stories woven into it. But why, I wonder, does it refer to the Isle of May? As we have already seen, the real Isle of May does have volcanic origins and, when seen from the mainland, it does lie where the water meets the sky. Its former villagers lived partly by tilling the soil, but mainly from the fruits of the sea. And, in the lighthouse, it does have a temple of stone constructed on its highest point.

But why should a fable about the Isle of May in the Firth if Forth (if indeed the story is about this island) have come to exist near San Francisco Bay in California, of all places?

No one in the hotel seemed to know, and I know of only one possible thread that might connect our Isle of May with Sausalito.

While the writer Robert Louis Stevenson (RLS) was still a young man, his father and others in the family tried to persuade him to follow the Stevenson family tradition and become a lighthouse engineer. His own real interests lay elsewhere, in the world of literature, and his far from robust health was another good reason for his not taking up such a profession. Despite this, his father's entreaties and threats cajoled young Robert Louis Stevenson into spending three of his summers supervising some of the family lighthouse projects. In 1868, when he was eighteen, he was based at Anstruther, involved with some work for his uncle, on the lighthouse on the Isle of May.

Young Louis seems not to have been over-enamoured either with the work or with Anstruther. In one of the letters that he sent from Fife to his mother he complained,

I am utterly sick of this grey, grim, sea-beaten hole. I have a little cold in my head, which makes my eyes sore; and you can't tell how utterly sick I am, and how anxious to get back among trees and flowers and some thing less meaningless than this bleak fertility.

Years later, Robert Louis Stevenson (RLS), now a renowned writer, met and fell in love with an American lady, Fanny Vandegrift Osbourne, who was separated from her husband. She later returned from Europe to America, but RLS, then aged 29, travelled to California to be with her. He arrived there ill and penniless, and initially eked out a living in Monterey and then San Francisco. By early 1880 Fanny had obtained a divorce and the couple finally got married. Their honeymoon was spent in a disused silver mine, only a few miles north of Sausalito. Until 1888 (when they left San Francisco to sail together to the South Seas, where RLS died in 1894) Robert and Fanny spent most of their time in California.

Did this great Scottish poet and writer perhaps, sometime during these years, leave behind him in Sausalito a mythical legend about Mikayla, based on the Isle of May he had known in his youth? Perhaps the reference that is made in the legend to the "statue in Mikayla's honour" was based on Stevenson's recollections of a panel of carved marble that still exists on one of the mantlepieces within the Tower. This depicts a "sea goddess" wearing a diaphanous gown, arising from the foam. She is borne on a scallop shell and being towed ashore by dolphins. If RLS had nothing to do with the Mikayla legend, what other explanation can there be for the unique name of this Scottish island in the middle of the Firth of Forth cropping up again, in a restaurant 6,000 miles away, in California?

Perhaps those unexplained footsteps that people in the Low Light occasionally hear, and the ghostly figure they have seen passing the window, are simply Mikayla, the Goddess of the Isle of May, returning from her "temple of stone" to her home in the off-shore depths of the North Sea.

*Could this carved figure on a marble mantlepiece in the
Tower lighthouse of the Isle of May have inspired the fable
about Mikayla, Goddess of the Isle of May, in Sausalito,
California?*

A second (and this time definitely factual) link between the Isle of May and the United States came to the author's notice in 2002, shortly after the second edition of this book went on sale. An American lady from Pennsylvania, Susan Ciccantelli, contacted me to ask if I could let her have any further information about the tragedy that happened on the Isle of May on January 25th 1791 at the original lighthouse beacon when seven people died in one night (see Chapter 6, page 40).   Her interest in that event was very understandable; she was the great-great-great-granddaughter of the infant girl who had been the sole survivor of the lighthouse keeper's family. She and I have since then jointly researched the subject, partly in Scotland and partly in the United States and a fascinating little story has emerged.

Lucy Dowie, née Anderson (from an album preserved by her granddaughter Margaret Acker, who lived to be 100 years old)

A search in the newspaper section of Edinburgh City Library produced a report that had appeared in the Edinburgh *Evening Courant* on Saturday January 29th 1791. This had been written by a Crail man and gave a graphic account of the tragedy. It seems that on a stormy Sunday evening, 23rd January, lighthouse keeper George Anderson and his family went to sleep, all together in one room of the beacon, leaving the two junior keepers to attend to the light until morning. At day-break on Monday morning these two men finished their duties and left the coal in the brazier of the light to burn itself out while they went to bed in an upper room of the beacon tower. On Monday evening people on the mainland were surprised when they saw that the light on the May was not lit as usual. Worries were expressed about what might have happened on the Island but, because of the stormy weather that continued to blow all through Tuesday, nobody was able to sail across to the Island to discover what was going on. Again on Tuesday night no light appeared and anxiety increased about what must have happened. However, the storm had abated sufficiently by Wednesday morning for one of the best boats in Crail to be manned and it set out for the Isle of May.

When the crew of this boat reached the beacon they found the door locked and were forced to break it down. The noise they created in doing this awakened one of the junior keepers who met them on the stair of the beacon, but he was in such a state of confusion he could tell the rescuers nothing about what had happened. They immediately went to the light keeper Anderson's room and were confronted by the sight of George Anderson and Elisabeth, his wife, in one bed, both dead, with an infant sucking at its dead mother's breast, scarcely alive. In another bed were five other children, three already dead and two unconscious and barely alive.

The cause of the deaths and unconsciousness appears to have been asphyxiation due to poisonous carbon monoxide and sulphur dioxide gases seeping into the rooms of the beacon. These gases came from the piles of ashes lying around the beacon, the residue of the coal fires that had been burned in its brazier every night. For years this refuse had simply been deposited alongside the building without giving any problem but on that fateful night some live coals from the brazier must have been showered down on top of the ashes by the strong gale that was blowing, and started a smouldering fire in them. It is almost certain that poisonous gases produced by the smouldering ashes were the cause of the tragedy.

The rescuers carefully carried the children who were still showing signs of life out of the beacon and into the fresh air, then took them and the two junior keepers to their boat and ferried them all back to Crail. The two junior keepers recovered fairly quickly, but one of the older children died in Crail on Thursday morning, despite having been given the best of attention there, and the other also died soon afterwards. The infant girl thus became the sole surviving member of the Anderson family other than two older sisters who lived on the mainland.

She was a little girl who had been christened Lucy Anderson in Crail Church in February 1790. According to local lore, she was looked after and brought up by the family of one of the men who had rescued her but other accounts say she was financially supported by the Scott family of Scotstarvit, near Cupar (who at that time were the owners of the Isle of May) and she may have been brought up by one of her sisters.

As confirmed by a scrutiny of Crail Old Parish records and the Scottish Government website, Lucy married one of the men who had sailed from Crail to rescue her, Henry Dowie. The wedding took place in 1806 in the same church in Crail where Lucy had been christened sixteen years earlier. Her husband was 23 years older than Lucy. His hometown was on the far side of Fife from the Isle of May, the village of Denbog near Auchtermuchty. The newly-weds seem to have set up house initially in that area, for their first son was born in Auchtermuchty although their second child was born in Anstruther, much closer to his mother's Isle of May birthplace.

In 1811 however, Mr and Mrs Henry Dowie decided to leave Scotland. They sailed with their two young sons (on the voyage Lucy was already pregnant with their third child) to the United States of America. By 1814 they had settled in

Susan Ciccantelli beside the Beacon where her great great great grandmother was the sole survivor of the tragedy that befell the Anderson family in 1791.

New York State on a farm near the small town of Andes in Delaware County. Lucy gave birth to ten more children in America, all of whom lived to become men and women. Henry became a successful dairy farmer and his Fife-born son (also Henry) built the first grist mill in the county. Lucy died there in 1845 and is remembered in an impressive memorial which was erected by her children on the farm where she spent the latter years of her life. On this obelisk Lucy is described as having had "a disposition in which every female virtue shone, pre-eminently a pattern of piety, patience and affection; invaluable as a mother, beloved as a friend and, for the last thirty years of her life, as a member of the M. E. Church of which she was an ornament." Henry died almost exactly a year later aged 77. Several of their descendants (starting with Sarah B Dowie, the youngest of their twelve children who crossed the Atlantic at the age of 70 in 1901) have visited Scotland, and at least two (John Douglas Dowie in 1982 and Susan Ciccantelli in 2003 and 2005) have sailed across the Firth of Forth to visit the old Beacon in a sort of pilgrimage to the place of their ancestor's birth (and so very nearly her death) on the Isle of May.

The memorial to Lucy and Henry Dowie erected in Andes, New York.

Bibliography

Bridges, Islands and Villages
of the Forth

Archibald, Malcolm (1990)

Collins Encyclopaedia
of Scotland

(Edited) John & Julia Keay (1994)

Exploring Scotland's Heritage
(Fife & Tayside)

Bruce Walker & Graham Ritchie
(HMSO - 1987)

One Man's Island

Brockie, Keith (1984)   (paintings and sketches)

Secrets of Fife's Holy Island

Yeoman, Peter
(Fife Archaeological Service)

The Isle of May

Eggeling, W.J.(1960)   (out of print)

The Lighthouse Stevensons

Bathurst, Bella (1999)

The "K" Boats

Everitt, D. E.

Acknowledgments

In writing this book I have been given a great deal of assistance and information by a large number of people. In this paragraph I express my gratitude to each and every one who has been involved with me in the preparation of this guide. Those whose contributions were particularly helpful included Ron Morris of Kirkcaldy, who shared with me his extensive knowledge of the May during WW2 ; Jimmy Aird of Peat Inn, who briefed me on many of the facts and inside information he has gleaned from his long experience of the Isle of May; Peter Yeoman and Douglas Spiers of Fife Archaeological Service who passed on specialist data concerning excavation works on the island etc. and also for permitting reproduction of the illustrations of the old beacon and priory; Caroline Gallacher of Scottish Natural Heritage, who put me right on the regulations concerning access to and activities permitted on the Isle of May; Rosalind Garton of Pitscottie, who provided me with some of the geological background about the island; John and Lisa Palmer of Cellardyke who shared with me some of their experiences of diving near the May; Nick Keir of Edinburgh, who kindly allowed me to quote from his song *Keepers;* Susan Ciccantelli, who helped research the history of Lucy Anderson after she survived the tragedy of 1791; Audrey Dishman of the Scottish Fisheries Museum, who first encouraged me to write this book; my wife Jane who showed great patience and forbearance during my months of obsession with the Isle of May, and who also undertook the proof-reading the book; and all the others who helped, each in his or her own way, to make this book possible.